# A SOLDIER IN GOD'S ARMY

*VICTORY OVER*
*the world, the flesh & the devil*

BY FRANK HUMMEL

ISBN 1-59352-045-X

Published by:
Christian Services Network
1975 Janich Ranch Ct.
El Cajon CA 92019
Toll Free: 1-866-6184



Printed in the United States of America

For more information contact:
The Publisher (see above)
Or
The Author (see page 133)

# CONTENTS

# FOREWORD

In these last days much has been written about spiritual warfare. What sets this work apart is the balanced presentation between the three enemies of the Christian's life, the devil, the flesh and the world. Frank Hummel is eminently qualified to write on this subject, not because of seminary degrees but as an overcoming veteran in the Lord's Army for over thirty years. Mr. Hummel was recognized in his field as an advertising executive and is known for his love for Christ and His Church. He is also a loving husband and father. His life is an example of being a man of God.

Having completed fifty years of ministry, thirty-four as a pastor, nine as a director of a ministerial fellowship and seven as professor at large in our denominational Bible Schools and Seminaries on the foreign field, I am pleased to recommend A SOLDIER IN GOD'S ARMY to the Body of Christ.

*J.R. Buskey*

J. R. Buskey,
B.A. M.Div. D.Min.

# PREFACE

According to my *prayer journal*, it was September 6, 1999 that the Holy Spirit dropped into my mind the idea for this book. In my quiet time that morning, the title, "A Soldier In God's Army", and the outline of nine aspects of spiritual warfare, were impressed upon me as a study of God's word which He wanted me to pursue. As I began this study, it soon became clear to me that I was to use the creative gifts God has given me to put this study in the form of a book. Since I've always enjoyed writing, this project became a blessing to me, as well as a learning experience.

Much has been written on the subject of *spiritual warfare*. The majority of it addresses the casting out of demons and dealing with the devil. Satan, however, is but one of the three major adversaries that Christians are confronted by every day - the other two being *the world* and *the flesh*. Paul identified all three of these enemies when he wrote, *"...you once walked according to the course of* ***this world****, according to the prince of the power of the air* ***(the devil)*** *the spirit who now works in the sons of disobedience, among whom also we all once conducted ourselves in the lusts of* ***our flesh****...."* (Eph. 2:2-3).

It is true: JESUS CHRIST WON THE ULTIMATE VICTORY FOR US ON CALVARY. Nevertheless, we as His followers, are engaged in an ongoing "mopping up" operation that involves us in spiritual warfare on a day to day basis. The purposes of this book are to help equip believers to better understand the nature of spiritual warfare, to identify the source or sources of the attacks against us, and to walk in the victory that has already been appropriated for us.

*A word of caution:* the subject of *spiritual warfare* is best understood by those in whom the Holy Spirit has taken up residence, as a result of inviting Jesus Christ into one's heart, as Lord and Savior. If you have never done this, perhaps now is the time to find a friend whom you know to be a sincere, committed Christian, to lead you through that process. Without the indwelling of the Holy Spirit, much of what follows will make little sense. It is my prayer that reading and applying the principles contained in this book will help you maintain a close walk with Jesus.

# ACKNOWLEDGEMENTS

So many teachers, pastors, authors and friends have influenced my thinking on spiritual warfare that it would be impossible to list them all here. A few are mentioned in this book. My heartfelt thanks to all of them. In addition, a special word of appreciation must go to the following:

Dr. Jack Buskey, a good friend and former pastor, who took time out of his busy schedule to review my manuscript and offer several helpful suggestions;

Rev. Ron Hill, another good friend who, while he was pastor of the Rocky Mount, VA Church of God (where we currently attend), reviewed the early chapters of the book, and offered much needed encouragement;

My wife, Betty, without whose love, sacrifice and encouragement I could never have undertaken this project.

Brothers and Sisters in Christ, who have taken the time to read this book and give me your feedback. Some of your kind remarks are listed on the back cover, and are a key reason we have decided to go with this second printing.

# DISCUSSION GUIDES

In the event that you are reading this book as part of a Sunday School class, a Bible study group, or just sharing it with another believer – or if you are reading it by yourself, and wish to apply it in your own life, there is a ***Discussion Guide*** at the end of each chapter. It is hoped that these ***Guides*** will better equip you, as a Soldier in God's Army, to walk in victory.

# PROLOGUE

It had been quite a week for Joshua. He had just led over 600,000 people across the Jordan River – on dry ground, no less, thanks to the mighty hand of God. He then directed the building of a memorial, using 12 stones taken from the middle of the river. Next was issuing the order for all the males to be circumcised, and supervising that bloody task.

It seemed only fitting then, for the people of God to celebrate their first Passover in the Promised Land. The day after the Passover, they ate some unleavened cakes and parched grain, the first produce yielded by their new homeland. Then the manna stopped – was God no longer going to provide for His people?

Now Joshua faced the seemingly insurmountable task of following the Lord's command to possess the land. Then a strange thing happened. Whether praying or in the midst of a power nap we are not sure; but he looked up and saw a man standing across from him dressed for battle and carrying a sword. No doubt with a good deal of trepidation, Joshua approached this awesome figure and asked if he was on their side or the enemy's. It is likely Joshua suspected this was some sort of divine visitation, but when the Warrior answered, *"No, rather I indeed come now as captain of the host of the Lord"*, there was no longer any doubt. Joshua fell on his face and worshipped Him.

*(continued on next page)*

Many biblical scholars agree that Joshua's encounter described above (Jos.5:13-15), is one of several Old Testament occurrences in which the second person of the Trinity, God the Son, revealed Himself to humans.

To think of Christ as a warrior is certainly consistent with the rest of scripture. Jesus himself said, *"I have not come to bring peace, but a sword"* (Mt. 10:34). In Revelation, He is seen waging war with a sharp, two-edged sword coming from His mouth (Re. 1:16; 2:16; 19:11-16). And it is not inconceivable that the army of horses and chariots of fire seen by Elisha and his servant (2 Kgs. 6:16-17), were under the command of the captain of the Lord's host, whom Joshua had encountered.

That spiritual warfare was a major part of the ministry of Jesus is clear. That Christians are to model their lives after Jesus is also clear. It is likely this is what He meant when He said, *"...the kingdom of heaven suffers violence, and violent men take it by force"* (Mt.11:12). It is also likely that this is what Paul and Barnabus had in mind when they encouraged the disciples with the words, *"Through many tribulations we must enter the kingdom of God"* (Acts 14:22). In short, spiritual warfare is not optional for the Christian, it is a way of life.

# CHAPTER ONE

## THE CALL TO ACTIVE DUTY

*"No soldier in active service entangles himself in the affairs of everyday life, so that he may please the one who enlisted him as a soldier."* 2 Tim.2:4.

"FROM THE PRESIDENT OF THE UNITED STATES, GREETINGS:" With these eight words, hundreds of thousands of men were called to active duty during the years that this country had a military draft. Chances are you will never receive a letter or telegram saying, "FROM THE CREATOR & REDEEMER OF THE UNIVERSE, GREETINGS:" But make no mistake about it, if you are a follower of Jesus, you have been called to active duty as a soldier in God's Army.

If you are wondering where that call is mentioned in scripture, consider the words of Peter who said, *"The promise is for you and...as many as the Lord our God shall **call** to Himself"* (Acts 2:39). And don't forget what Paul said about God working all things together for good for those who are ***called*** according to His purposes (Ro.8:28). Finally, with the words of Jesus, *"Many are **called**, but few are chosen"* (Mt.22:14), it becomes evident that God's call is to all mankind, but only those who respond positively to Him will be selected to become His soldiers.

To better understand what it means to be called to be a soldier in God's army, let's look at some of the elements common to His call to several of His soldiers.

**<u>God makes the call clear.</u>** With Moses, God used a burning bush to get his attention. And once Moses turned aside to check it out, there could be no doubt in his mind that God was calling him for a special purpose (Ex.3:2-6).

It was a little easier for God to get Joshua's attention. Joshua had served under Moses, and learned much from him. So when God instructed Moses to transfer some of his authority to Joshua, it was clear that Joshua was being called to continue what God had called Moses to do – lead His people into the Promised Land (Nu.27:18-23). After Moses died, God spoke directly to Joshua, confirming his call and giving specific instructions (Jos.1:1-9).

Then there was Gideon. This poor chap must have suffered from poor self image, inferiority complex, and nagging doubt, all rolled into one. When God called him, he asked for a sign (Judg.6:11-21), which God clearly gave him. Still questioning God, he later set a fleece before God, not once, but twice, to reassure himself that God was still in control. Christians today should be very careful about "fleecing", but God made it clear to Gideon that he was being called.

The classic New Testament example of God making his call clear is with Paul (Acts 9:1-20). A zealous follower of God, Saul had to be knocked off his horse for God to get his attention. But once He had it, the Lord found Saul (later to become Paul) to be a committed soldier in the Army of God. His call was clear.

For David Wilkerson, a country preacher from Pennsylvania, God used a photo in LIFE Magazine to get his attention. In 1958, as Wilkerson gazed at the picture of a hardened teenager caught up in the gang warfare and drug abuse which were rampant in New York City, he knew God was calling him to go to New York to reach out to these young people with the life changing power of the gospel. His call was clear, and resulted in the founding of Teen Challenge, an extremely successful drug rehabilitation program, which today has over 130 centers in the U.S. and internationally. This true-life Christian adventure is told in the exciting book, THE CROSS AND THE SWITCHBLADE[i], which was later made into a movie starring actor Pat Boone playing the role of Dave Wilkerson.

**God outlines the mission and the plan.** "*I will send you to Pharaoh*", said God to Moses, "*so that you may bring My people out of Egypt.*" Not only did God give Moses the mission, but He also issued explicit instructions on how to go about accomplishing the task (Ex.3:10-22). The same was true with Joshua. When God called him to lead His people into the Promised Land, He also gave him the plan for doing it (Jos.3:8-13). And so it was with Gideon. When God called him to defeat the

Midianites, He gave him detailed instructions for selecting his army (Judg.7:1-8). Paul's mission to carry the Gospel to the gentiles was clearly outlined for him by God, through a disciple named Ananias (Acts 9:10-19). Every soldier in God's army is given a mission, usually accompanied by a plan to carry it out.

**God is serious about His call.** When God calls a soldier, He means business. With Moses and Joshua, God instructed them to remove their shoes because they were on Holy Ground. There is a good deal of symbolism in the removal of one's shoes. In 1995, I attended a Promise Keepers Conference in Atlanta. Pastor, songwriter, and author Jack Hayford was one of the speakers. Describing the call of Moses, Hayford pointed out the following (according to my notes):

> *The shoes, which have a sole, represent our human soul, which is so easily stained by the world; shoes also represent the work of our hands, our own resources (we earned the money to buy them); furthermore, shoes elevate us, when we need to be brought low. So God says don't be stained by the world; rely on My resources, not your own; and humble yourself by totally relying on Me. I'm serious about this – get rid of the shoes.*

Hayford concluded his message by asking over 60,000 men to remove their shoes to show they were serious about God's call on their lives.

With Paul, God took a different approach. Paul was blinded for three days, which definitely let him know that God wasn't just fooling around. When God calls a soldier, it should never be taken lightly.

**God provides the means for accomplishing the mission.** Most of us are like Gideon. He knew he wasn't qualified to do what God called him to do. So, God assured him that He would be with him, and then confirmed this fact through signs and wonders (Judg.6:15-21; 36-40). Moses felt the same way. So God infused his staff with supernatural power, and gave him Aaron as a spokesman (Ex.4:2-17). Any soldier who feels he *is* qualified to engage in spiritual warfare is probably on shaky ground at best. Jesus made it clear that without Him, we can do nothing (Jn.15:5). God's provision for today's Christian soldier is outlined in the chapter entitled *The Weapons of Our Warfare.*

**God removes us from our "comfort zone".** Moses had it made. After leaving Egypt as a young man, he spent the next 40 years in Midian. He had married into a wealthy family, and was shepherding the flock of his father-in-law, Jethro. When God called him, he knew he had to ask Jethro to release him for that call (Ex.4:18).

Peter, Andrew, James and John were successful commercial fishermen. When Jesus called them to become *fishers of men*, they followed Him without hesitation, knowing it meant leaving their boats and nets behind (Mt.4:18-22).

The same was true of David Wilkerson, who left the security of a good job in a peaceful rural community to answer God's call to minister to drug addicts and prostitutes on the streets of New York City. It is known as *the way of the cross.* And when Jesus speaks to His followers about taking up their cross, He is talking about forsaking the past for a new and better life serving God.

You may never see a burning bush or be knocked off a horse. And your call may be less dramatic than leading a nation into the Promised Land. Perhaps you've been asked to teach a Sunday school class, or go on a short-term mission trip. Maybe as you've prayed for a neighbor, the Holy Spirit has impressed you to reach out to the needy around you in tangible ways.

Your call to active duty, whether it be to sing in the church choir, or direct a world-wide ministry, will require the qualities of character spelled out in the following acrostic – and then some.

**C** – Consecration: knowing you have been set apart for God's work;
**A** – Abandonment: totally forsaking the old life (both good and bad);
**L** – Loyalty: placing God's plans and purposes above everything else;
**L** – Leadership: setting an example of obedience and submission to God's authority by being a servant.

In his book, PURSUEING THE WILL OF GOD[ii], Jack Hayford says, "*The Lord's call is to you. His will is for you. The people around you may or may not feel comfortable and easy about where's He's calling you to go and what He's calling you to do. But it's the Lord to whom you must answer, and He is the One who not only knows the end from the beginning, He knows you better than you know yourself.*"

~~~~~~~~~~~

**DISCUSSION GUIDE**
**FOR CHAPTER ONE**

1. When did God call you to active duty?

2. How did His call change your life?

3. Do you think Gideon was wrong to question God's will by using fleeces?

4. What assignment(s) has God given to you as a soldier in His Army?

5. Has God's call on your life removed you from your "comfort zone"? If yes, how? If no, what do you think it will take?

6. Rate yourself on a scale of 1 to 5 (1 being weak, and 5 being strong) on each of the CALL traits: (see page 6)

| | **my score** |
|---|---|
| **C**onsecration | __________ |
| **A**bandonment | __________ |
| **L**oyalty | __________ |
| **L**eadership | __________ |
~~~~~~~~~~~

## ENDNOTES

---

[i] THE CROSS AND THE SWITCHBLADE – by David Wilkerson, John and Elizabeth Sherrill
Copyright © 1962 – David Wilkerson
Berkley Publishing Group – May 1976

[ii] PURSUEING THE WILLOF GOD - by Jack Hayford
Copyright © 1997
Publisher: Multnomah Publishers, Inc. PO Box 1720, Sisters, OR 97759

# CHAPTER TWO

## PUTTING ON THE UNIFORM

*"For all of you who were baptized into Christ have clothed yourselves with Christ."* Galatians 3:27.

"You're out of uniform, soldier." Those harsh and critical words have been addressed to many a GI over the years, in a variety of circumstances. "Hawkeye" Pierce, the fictional hero of the MASH television series, was frequently accused of that because of his preference for wearing casual civilian clothes rather than the expected military garb.

In the real world, something as minor as wearing an unauthorized cap, insignia or service ribbon could easily result in such a reprimand. While it may seem picayune, the military relies quite heavily on being able to identify its members at a glance, if for no other reason than to be able to tell what branch of the service, or what unit the one wearing the uniform represents.

Christians wear a uniform too. In the early 1970's, when I was involved with the Full Gospel Business Men's Fellowship, I often had the pleasure of picking up our guest speakers at the airport. On one such occasion, when I was supposed to pick up Arthur Katz, I was delayed in traffic. Upon arriving at the terminal, I discovered that his plane had already landed. Though Art had never met me, I knew his appearance from pictures I had seen, so was sure I could find him. To my surprise, as I walked down the corridor toward the gate at which his flight had arrived, I saw Art, pointing at me, while talking to the man next to him. When I greeted him, Art explained that the man with whom he was talking had asked how he would recognize me. Art had told him that most Christians have a distinctive countenance about them; and when he saw me, he pointed at me and said, "There he is."

We may not be aware of it, as Moses was not aware of his shining (Ex. 34:29), but all believers walking in His light have this countenance. And while our countenance may not always be sufficient to identify us as soldiers in God's army, there are a number of qualities with which a follower of Jesus should be clothed. Among these are the following:

**Humility.** *"Clothe yourselves with humility,"* writes Peter (1 Pe.5:5). *"Put on ... humility,"* says Paul (Col. 3:12). These are but two of many references found in the epistles, which endorse the teachings and lifestyle of Jesus, found in the gospels. It is interesting to note that Paul and Peter use terminology such as *clothe* and *put on* when it comes to showing humility in our lives. Perhaps that's because humility does not come naturally for most of us. It is something that requires a conscious decision to act in a way that considers others as more important than self.

Such terminology also recognizes that most of us have a natural pride that needs to be replaced with genuine, godly humility. That's probably where the humorous antidote came from that tells of the man who received a medal for *humility;* they had to take it away from him because he wore it.

And our humility must be before both God and men. Author Andrew Murray put it this way: *"It is easy to think that we humble ourselves before God: humility before men will be the only sufficient proof that our humility before God is real..."*[i]

The importance of humility in spiritual warfare is emphasized by James, when after telling us we should resist the devil, he says, *"Humble yourselves in the presence of the Lord"* (Ja. 4:7-10).

**Light.** *"Put on the armor of light,"* says Paul (Ro. 13:12). We are exhorted throughout scripture to walk in the light, be children of light, and to let our light shine. Jesus told His followers, *"You are the light of the world...let your light shine before men that they may see your good works and glorify your Father in heaven."* The wonderful thing about light is that it extinguishes darkness. We all have areas of darkness in our lives; they are called *sin.* Putting on light, therefore, involves dealing with the sin in our lives. John puts this all together for us in his first epistle when he writes, *"...God is light, and in Him there is no darkness at all...but if we walk in the light as He Himself is in the light, we have fellowship with one another, and the blood of Jesus His Son cleanses us from all sin"* (1 Jn.1:5-9).

**Love.** In his letter to the Colossians, Paul writes, *"... beyond all these things, put on love..."*. The *"all these things"* Paul refers to includes what he has written just ahead of this, namely, *"...put on a heart of compassion, kindness, humility, gentleness and patience..."* (Col.3:12-14). Love is a common theme of Paul's writings, the most notable passage being 1 Corinthians 13, where he again equates love to a lifestyle that demonstrates compassion, humility, patience, gentleness and other fruit of the Spirit. It is in this famous passage that Paul makes two profound statements about love: first, *"love never fails"*; and second, *"the greatest of these* (all Christian virtues) *is love"* (1 Cor.13:8, 13).

Though I am not a linguistic scholar, it is my understanding that there are at least three different Greek words used to convey the meaning of love. One is *phileo,* (used often in the New Testament) which refers to a brotherly type of love.

Another is *eros,* which is not found in the Bible. This is the root from which we get the word *erotic,* and usually has a sexual or sensual connotation. The literal meaning of *eros,* however, is a love that expects something in return (you scratch my back, and I'll scratch yours).

The third is *agape,* a word used frequently by Jesus. *Agape* is an unconditional love, expecting nothing in return. Guess which kind of love we are supposed to put on. That's right - *agape.*

As with *putting on humility,* we find that *putting on love* is not a natural act; it involves going beyond the natural, walking in the Spirit, in the realm of the supernatural. And as with *putting on light,* it involves dealing with sin in our lives; for the scriptures say, *"...love covers a multitude of sins"* (1 Pe.4:8). Little wonder that *love* is an essential part of the uniform of a soldier in God's army.

**The New Self.** Paul tells us to *"put on the new self"* (Eph.4:24, Col.3.10). He also tells us to *put off, or lay aside, the old self* (Eph.4:22). So what is he talking about here? One of the most quoted scriptures on this subject is 2 Corinthians 5:17, *"...if any man is in Christ, he is a new creature; the old things passed away; behold, new things have come."* Make no mistake about it, when you receive Jesus Christ as your Lord and savior, this becomes an instant reality – you **are** a new creature in Christ. That's the spiritual side of it.

The natural side is that the old man dies hard – the flesh doesn't like to give up. Chapters five through eight of Romans give a thorough explanation of the struggle between the old self and the new self, along with instructions on how to be victorious. An important key to being victorious is Romans 6:11, *"...consider yourselves to be dead to sin, but alive to God in Christ Jesus."* This becomes a matter of a daily walk with Him, in which we make choices to please God, rather than our old sinful nature. No doubt, this is what Jesus meant when He told those who wish to follow Him that it would involve denying self and taking up a cross (Mt.16:24). Jesus used the illustration of a yoke (Mt.11:29-30), which suggests a side by side partnership arrangement. Paul expresses this well when he writes, *"...work out your salvation with fear and trembling, for it is God who is at work in you, both to will and to work for His good pleasure"* (Ph.2:12-13).

**The Lord Jesus Christ.** One of the latest Christian fads involves jewelry, clothing, bookmarks and other items with the initials **WWJD** (What Would Jesus Do?). Taken from the Christian classic, IN HIS STEPS, by Charles M. Sheldon[ii], this phrase encourages believers to follow the exhortation of Paul in Romans 13:14, *"...put on the Lord Jesus Christ."* In this part of his letter to the Romans, Paul urges his readers to *"...lay aside the deeds of darkness and put on the armor of light...and make no provision for the flesh in regards to its lusts."* In other words, in every situation try to think what Jesus would do, and then respond in obedience by doing what is pleasing to God.

A favorite scripture of many believers is Romans 8:28, which explains that *God works all things together for good for those who love Him,* and *are called according to His purpose.* The very next verse explains what *His* purpose is: *that we might be conformed to the image of His son, that He might be the first-born among many brethren.*

Does this mean we lose our own personality and

individuality? No way!! It does mean, however, that more and more we find our identity *in Christ*, as members of *His body*, as *His ambassadors* (2 Cor.5:20) or representatives.

Jesus himself said, *"He who receives you receives Me..."* (Mt.10:40), and *"The one who listens to you listens to Me..."*. As you put on the Lord Jesus Christ (making Him part of your uniform as a soldier in God's army), you will find that it results in both blessings and hardships.

The blessings include love, joy, peace and the other fruit of the Spirit in your life, to say nothing of the eternal inheritance that belongs to all those who are *in Christ*. The hardships include the various trials and sufferings that result from taking up our cross and following Him. Both the blessings and the hardships are essential if we are to walk in victory.

**Insignia.** The military uses insignia to identify such things as branch of service, rank, assigned unit, etc. In Genesis 17 we read that God directed Abram to place an insignia on every male descendant of his to show that they were a part of God's covenant people. It was the mark of circumcision, and while this insignia was not visible to the general public, it was nevertheless visible to God – and important to Him. So much so that before the battle of Jericho, He instructed Joshua to circumcise all the male Israelites who had not received the mark of the covenant during the 40 years in the wilderness (Josh.5:2-8).

From scriptures like Deuteronomy 10:16, Jeremiah 4:4 and Romans 2:29, however, it becomes clear that the insignia God is looking for on His soldiers today is not a circumcision of the flesh, but a *circumcised heart. "For the eyes of the Lord move to and fro throughout the earth that He may strongly support those whose heart is completely His"* (2 Chr.16:9).

Putting on the uniform of a soldier in God's army would not be complete without referring to the well-known passage that speaks about *putting on the whole armor of God* (Eph.6:11-17). It is interesting to note that the only offensive weapon listed in this passage is the *sword of the Spirit,* which is the word of God. The other items which represent *truth, righteousness, the gospel of peace, and faith,* are all for defensive purposes. It should also be noted that while this passage deals primarily with warfare against Satan and demonic forces, the same set of armor will be needed in battles against *the world* and *the flesh.* This passage will be addressed further in Chapter 6, The Weapons Of Our Warfare.

So, you've been called as a soldier in God's army. You've put on a uniform consisting of:

> Humility, which considers others as more important than self;
>
> Light, which causes you to forsake sin;

Love, which seeks nothing in return;

A new self, which considers "the old self" to be dead;

The Lord Jesus Christ, which constantly asks the question, "What Would Jesus Do?"

and The Insignia of a circumcised heart.

And let it never be said of you, "You're out of uniform, soldier." Now it's time to get ready for Basic Training.

~~~~~~~~~~~

**DISCUSSION GUIDE FOR CHAPTER TWO**

1. Of the six items (Humility, Light, Love, The New Self, The Lord Jesus Christ, the Insignia) making up the uniform, which is the most difficult for you to put on? Why?

2. Which is the easiest for you to put on? Why?

3. What do you think God is asking you to do to keep from being "out of uniform"?
~~~~~~~~~~~

## ENDNOTES

---

[i] HUMILITY – The Beauty of Holiness - by Andrew Murray
Flemming H. Revell Co., Old Tappan, NJ 07675
Marshall, Morgan and Scott
Blundell House, Goodwood Rd., London SE14 6BL
Printed in 1961; reprinted in 1965 and 1972

[ii] IN HIS STEPS – by Charles M. Sheldon
Copyright © 1962
Published by: Guideposts Associates, Inc., Carmel, NY

# CHAPTER THREE

## BASIC TRAINING

*"...discipline yourself for the purpose of godliness; for bodily discipline is only of little profit, but godliness is profitable for all things, since it holds promise for the present life and also for the life to come."* 1 Timothy 4:7-8.

BIOC (Basic Infantry Officers Course) at Fort Benning, GA lasted four months – January through April, 1955. The first couple of weeks were the toughest, as those of us who were married had to leave the comfort of our off-base housing, and bunk with the single guys in austere military barracks. While it was probably less severe than the "boot camp" training that enlisted men endured, it was nevertheless an intensive 120 days.

We had daily calisthenics (the old "Army Daily Dozen") along with extended periods of jogging. They taught us tactics and strategy 'til they were coming out our ears. We learned how to assemble, disassemble, clean, care for and use our weapons (mostly the old M-1 rifle). We learned how to blow up bridges, call in armor and artillery fire, use night vision equipment (yes, they even had that high tech stuff back in the 50's), ride in helicopters, do hand-to-hand combat, use a bayonet, and much, much more.

Fortunately, most of us never had to use the information and skills we had acquired under combat conditions. The Korean conflict had ended in 1953, and except for a few who made a career of the military, we were too old to see action in Vietnam.

Basic training for the soldier in God's Army, however, is **not** an experience that may or may not be put to use. <u>It is absolutely essential for survival</u>.

The military recognizes that, even though everything taught may not be put to use, it is in basic training that *discipline* is developed. The writer of Proverbs says, "*He who neglects discipline despises himself*" (Pr.15:32). Paul points out in 1 Corinthians 9:24-27, those who are successful spiritually as well as physically, attain victory only through *discipline.* And certainly, when Jesus stated that the greatest commandment is to *love God with all your heart, soul, mind and strength* (Mt.22:36-40), one cannot help but see that this requires great *discipline.*

At the risk of over simplifying things, we will examine four disciplines that should be part of the basic training, as well as the ongoing experience, of every soldier on God's Army: 1)The Word; 2)Prayer; 3)Praise and Worship; and 4)Fellowship. But first, a story:

It was one of those typically dreary Saturday mornings in central New York. It was early April, 1971. The temperature was in the low forties, with a threat of rain. Since I had been trying to work out at least three times a week, and I had been able to get two workouts in so far that week, it looked like now was the time to do it if I was to achieve my goal for the week. My workout consisted of a few light calisthenics plus a strenuous 20 to 30 minute bike ride.

But something was in the way -- a prior commitment. It had been two and a half years since God had met me in such a meaningful way on a New Hampshire hillside, and I had committed my life to Jesus Christ. And it wasn't long after that life changing experience that the Holy Spirit impressed upon me the importance of spending the first part of each day in communion with the Lord -- through prayer, meditation, scripture reading, or some combination of these activities. This delightfully rewarding discipline was relatively easy to put into practice Monday through Friday; all I had to do was set the alarm about an hour earlier than normal to allow time before going to work.

But Saturdays were different. Saturday was my day, to do what I wanted; whether cleaning out the garage, playing tennis, going fishing, or just plain loafing. Thus my dilemma on that dreary Saturday. Do I obey the Lord, or try to beat the rain by going for a morning bike ride?

After a brief and typically one-sided conversation with the Lord, I decided to "make a deal" with God: I would pray while I rode my bike. Praying while riding a bike is difficult even under ideal conditions. So with the potential malfunctions of my ancient three-speed Schwinn, coupled with the hazards of neighborhood vehicular traffic, it was virtually impossible. Nevertheless, I was soon doing my thing, peddling my trusty cycle down the road. Within five minutes, I happened to notice a large dog crouching on the front porch of a neighbor's house. At about the same time, the dog happened to notice me, and apparently concluded that I was trying to invade his turf. With a few short but swift bounds, he was running along side the rear wheel of my bike. With one more bound, he was grasping my sweat pants, with his teeth penetrating the flesh of my gluteus maximus. His mission accomplished, the dog returned home, as did I.

After going to the doctor for a tetanus booster, I was subjected to the further humiliation of having to relate the incident to a police officer who had been notified by the doctor. This in turn led to an embarrassing confrontation with the dog's owner. These unplanned and unpleasant Saturday morning activities accomplished, it was time to repent. Since my morning quiet times had recently been spent reading the epistles of Paul, I decided as penance I would read all the "Ts"; 1st and 2nd Thessalonians, 1st and 2nd Timothy, and Titus. Now it was God's turn to speak, and speak He did.

When I came to 1st Timothy 4:8 in my Phillips New Testament, He said, *"Bodily fitness has limited value, but spiritual fitness is of unlimited value, for it holds promise both for this present life and for the life to come."* The message couldn't have been clearer. I got the point, in more ways than one. That evening, as my wife Betty and I were kneeling beside the bed in prayer, I began to chuckle. "What are you laughing at?" she asked. "Well," I responded, "in the story of Jonah it says, *'the Lord appointed a big fish.'* But in my case, the Lord appointed a big dog."

~~~~~~~~~~~

Now let's examine the four basic disciplines mentioned earlier.

**The Word.** In a letter to Timothy, the apostle Paul states that *"All scripture is inspired by God,*
~~~~~~~~~~~

*and is profitable for teaching, reproof, correction, and for training in righteousness*" (2 Tim. 3:16). So, daily Bible reading , meditating on the Word, and scripture memorization all help to equip us for spiritual warfare.

The discipline of the Word is an effective weapon against all three of our spiritual enemies: Psalm 1 tells us that the person who meditates daily on the Word of God will be victorious over the ungodly influences of *the world.* Hebrews 4:12 points out that the Word of God enables us to separate spiritual thinking from that which is soulish, or of *the flesh.* And in Luke 4:1-13, we have a graphic picture of Jesus using the Word to counter the attacks of *the devil.*

Here are a few tips that may help make your discipline in the Word more fruitful and enjoyable:

1. Read for content, to learn the story of how God has worked and related to man throughout history - who were the heroes and villains?; what did they do?; what did God do? etc.

2. Meditate on the word. Don't be in a hurry. *This is different than reading for content.* Allow the Holy Spirit to be your teacher. Several years ago, I spent a month or more meditating on 1 Corinthians 13, asking the Lord to help me improve in the area of love. More recently, I spent a few weeks reading nothing but the first 12 verses of John 15, with a prayerful desire to

learn how to *"abide in Christ"*. Meditating on these two passages of scripture has had a profound impact on my relationship with God.

3. Memorize scripture. This will help you reinforce spiritual principles and truths by which to live. It will also enable you to share God's Word with others in a spontaneous manner.

4. Vary your reading. While it is a good idea to set goals for how much to read and/or memorize, be careful not to get legalistic about this. (Legalism in this area can result in a loss of joy and/or the sin of pride.) So spend some time reading for content, some for memorization, and some just meditating on the Word.

5. Make notes in your Bible. Underline and highlight passages that are meaningful to you.

6. Try a new translation every year or two. If the King James or some other translation is sacred to you, fine. But several of the more contemporary translations such as the NIV (New International Version) and the NAS (New American Standard) are generally true to the original manuscripts, and often easier to understand.

For the soldier in God's Army, spending time in The Word on a daily basis extends beyond basic training; it becomes an essential part of our ongoing life in Christ. In Chapter 6, we will discuss more about how to use The Word as a weapon for spiritual warfare.

**Prayer.** In the classic devotional, MY UTMOST FOR HIS HIGHEST[i], the late Oswald Chambers says, *"Prayer does not fit us for the greater works; prayer* ***is*** *the greater work."* Chambers also says, *"If we think of prayer as the breath in our lungs and the blood from our hearts, we think rightly. The blood flows ceaselessly, and breathing continues ceaselessly; we are not conscious of it, but it is always going on. Prayer is not an exercise, it is the life."* These quotes help us understand what Paul meant when he said we are to *pray without ceasing* (1 Th. 5:17). An excellent little book (less than 100 pages) on this concept is THE PRACTICE OF THE PRESENCE OF GOD,[ii] by Brother Lawrence.

So, what exactly is prayer? A simple definition would be to say that prayer is communication with God. This suggests that at least half of the time we devote to prayer should be spent listening. (After all, God gave us two ears and only one mouth). Well known author and teacher, Henry Blackaby has said that what God says to us in prayer is far more important than what we say to Him[iii]. Psalm 46:10 says, *"Be still and know that I am God."*

Being still before the Lord, or spending time just quietly *waiting upon the Lord,* as suggested in Isaiah 40:31, is probably the most difficult part of the discipline of prayer. When learned and practiced, however, it becomes not only a means of hearing God's voice, but a tremendous source of blessing as we are renewed with His life and His strength, while we abide in His presence.

The verbal portion of prayer, what we say to God, can take many forms. New believers often struggle with finding the "proper" method; even Jesus' disciples asked Him to teach them how to pray. His response was to give them a model which we have come to know as "The Lord's Prayer." While there is nothing wrong with praying the Lord's prayer verbatim, it is important to remember that it was intended to be a model that individual believers can adapt to their own situation. Some have modified this into what is often called the ACTS formula:

A - adoration
C - confession
T – thanksgiving
S – supplication

Whatever form our prayers take, they should be sincere, honest and specific. There are numerous prayers in both the Old and New Testaments (Psalms is an especially good source) which offer still more guidelines on how and what to pray for. There are also many books on prayer that can be helpful. One that has been a blessing to many is THE PRAYER OF JABEZ[iv] by Bruce Wilkinson.

Prayer can be corporate or individual. Both should be a regular activity for every soldier in

God's Army; corporate prayer at least once a week (most likely with fellow believers at a regularly scheduled service), and individual prayer on a daily basis. At the beginning of our discussion on prayer we addressed the idea of *praying without ceasing,* or maintaining ongoing communication with God. While this may be the essence of individual prayer, it is nevertheless essential that the Soldier in God's Army set aside specific times to pray every day. Jesus refers to these times as *"prayer closet"* praying (Mt. 6:6).

Some of the specific ways that prayer (both individual and corporate) can be used in our battles against *the world, the flesh* and *the devil* will be discussed in Chapter 6, The Weapons of Our Warfare.

**Praise and Worship.** Most Christians think of praise and worship as something you do when you "go to church". (Unfortunately, some don't even think of it as a church activity.) In the book of Numbers, several references are made to the *daily* offerings and sacrifices which God instructed His people to perform as an act of praise and worship.

Numerous Psalms and frequent references in the prophetic books give further support for the fact that the Lord expects His people to praise and worship Him on a *daily* basis. Acts 2:46-47 tells us that part of the *daily* activities of the early church was *"praising God"*. Although we may have scheduled times for praise and worship, it can also be spontaneous, as was the case with Paul and Silas when they ended up in a Philippian jail (see Acts 16:23-25).

Is there a difference between praise and worship? *Praise* means to exalt, glorify and honor God by what we do or say. *Worship* can be defined as the expression of an intense love, admiration and adoration of God. Musically speaking, *praise* is often thought of as upbeat rhythms and songs that tell **about** God's great feats and attributes, while *worship* consists of slower melodies with lyrics sung **to** God expressing our love and devotion to Him.

Our purpose here is not to establish a definition or prescribe a formula, but simply to encourage a daily pattern that includes a supernaturally, natural flow of praise and worship to God for *Who He Is* and *what He has done.*

While this is not intended to be a thorough treatise on the subject, there are some basic questions which scripture answers for us about praise and worship. These include:

<u>Who should do it?</u> – Every believer (Ps. 150:6.

<u>When should we do it?</u> - All the time (Phil. 4:4; He.13:15; Ps. 34:1).

<u>How should we do it?</u> - Speaking, singing, clapping, lifting hands, dancing, shouting, etc. (Eph. 5:19-20; Ps.150:3-5; Ps.47.1; Ps.66:1; Ps.32.11).

Why should we do it? - He is worthy of our praise and worship (Rev.4:11; 5:12).

Where should we do it? – In church, in the world, everywhere (Ps.150:1; 1 Tim. 2:8).

One final word on praise and worship: the word is *sacrifice.* Hebrews 13:15-16 points out that *"the sacrifice of praise"* involves not only the fruit of our lips, but also doing good and sharing. In Romans 12:1, Paul tells us to present our bodies *"as a living sacrifice"*, which is *"a spiritual service of worship."*

When Jesus told His followers to take up their cross daily, He was simply referring to the act of willingly and joyfully choosing to do what pleases God, rather than what pleases ourselves. This is the ultimate act of praise and worship.

If you're getting the idea here that our *basic training* disciplines seem to carry over to our entire Christian walk, then you are getting the right picture. And for the soldier in God's Army, there is one more discipline to learn – fellowship.

**Fellowship.** God says, *"It is not good for man to be alone..."* (Gen.2:18). That's why He created Eve. It stands to reason, that since He created mankind in His own image that the Lord must have had in mind the idea of having someone with whom He could fellowship.

In spite of all the training we give our children

on the importance of becoming *independent*, to say nothing of the value the world places on *independence*, the fact remains that we are *interdependent*. We need each other.

The heartfelt cry of Jesus in His high priestly prayer was that we may all be ONE, just as He and the Father are ONE (Jn.17:21). In 1 Cor.12:12-25, Paul elaborates on how we can have this kind of spiritual unity in spite of our many differences of gifts, talents and callings. Christian fellowship is the key to bringing about the answer to Jesus' prayer for unity.

John Poole, a well known Bible teacher during the early 1970's used to describe what passes for fellowship in many churches, contrasted with the kind of fellowship God wants us to have. His description went something like this:

> "Hi. How are you?"
> "Fine. How are you?"
> "Fine. How's the wife?"
> "Fine. How about yours?"
> "She's fine, too. How are the kids?
> "They're fine. How about yours?"
> "They're fine. How's the dog?"
> etc., etc., etc.

This is what Poole described as "*marble fellowship*", where we come together and bounce off each other like marbles, without any real involvement in one another's lives. According to

Poole, you might as well cut right to the bottom line and start out by asking, "*How's the dog?*"

His term for the type of fellowship God wants us to have is *"grape fellowship"*. This is where we come together and allow the Holy Spirit to squeeze us like a bunch of grapes, our very lives being intermingled with one another, making us into a sweet new wine that is pleasing to Him.

Throughout the book of Acts (especially 2:44-47) we see some beautiful pictures of *"Grape fellowship"*. The epistles give us further insights into what true Christian fellowship is, and how it works. A few examples:

> "...*speaking the truth in love*..." (Eph.4:15)
> "...*be subject to one another*..." (Eph.5:21)
> "...*regard one another as more important than one's self*..." (Phil.2:3)
> "...*bear one another's burdens*..." (Ga.6:2)
> "...*stimulate one another to love and good deeds*..." (Heb.10:24)

There are many more, but 1 John 1:7 sums it up nicely by saying, *"...if we walk in the light as He Himself is in the light, we have fellowship with one another..."*

There are many forms of fellowship available to the soldier in God's Army. The most obvious are regular church meetings (Sunday morning and evening worship services, etc.). There are also opportunities such as neighborhood Bible studies and prayer meetings; accountability groups (a concept promoted by Promise Keepers to help men lead more Godly lives); home groups (often called cell groups or life groups); and day to day contact with Christian friends.

A word of caution: it is almost impossible to avoid having fellowship with the world. This is not necessarily bad (how else will we reach the world for Jesus?). If you're on a bowling team, your fellowship is centered around bowling. If you have a job, your fellowship is centered around your work. Your Christian fellowship, whether a recreational activity, a church service, or whatever, should always be centered on Jesus Christ; after all, He is there in your midst (Mt.18:20). And like the other disciplines (The Word, Prayer, and Praise & Worship), Fellowship must be exercised on a regular basis.

Having received your call, put on the uniform, and completed your basic training, it's now time to consider the qualifications required for promotion as a soldier in God's Army.

~~~~~~~~~~~
~~~~~~~~~~~

## DISCUSSION GUIDE FOR CHAPTER THREE

1. On a scale of 1 to 10 (10 being excellent), rate yourself on the four Basic Training Disciplines:

| Discipline | My Score |
|---|---|
| The Word | _______ |
| Prayer | _______ |
| Praise & Worship | _______ |
| Fellowship | _______ |

2. What steps do you believe God wants you to take to bring each score up to a 10?

ENDNOTES

---

[i] MY UTMOST FOR HIS HIGHEST by Oswald Chambers
Copyright © 1935
Publisher: Dodd, Mead & Company - New York, NY

[ii] THE PRACTICE OF THE PRESENCE OF GOD by Brother Lawrence
Copyright © 1958,1967 Fleming H. Revel
Publisher: Spire Books, Div. Of Baker Book House
Grand Rapids, MI

[iii] EXPERIENCING GOD – Knowing and Doing The Will Of God,
by Henry T. Blackaby and Claude V. King
Copyright © 1990
Publisher: LifeWay Press – 127 Ninth Ave., North
Nashvlle, TN 37234

[iv] THE PRAYER OF JABEZ by Dr. Bruce H. Wilkinson
Copyright © 2000 by Bruce H. Wilkinson
Publisher: Multnomah Publishers, Inc.
PO Box 1720, Sisters, OR 97759

# CHAPTER FOUR

## QUALIFICATIONS FOR PROMOTION

*"For promotion cometh neither from the east, nor from the west, nor from the south. But God is the judge: He putteth down one and setteth up another."* Psalm 75:6-7 (KJV).

The first time I met Merle Allender, he was a West Virginia hillbilly who delighted in strumming gospel tunes with a country beat on his trusty guitar, belting out the inspiring lyrics, and reaching out to everyone around him with the love of Jesus. He was also a Major in the United States Marine Corp. He had flown several combat missions during the Korean conflict, and was a decorated war hero. When he spoke at the Syracuse, NY Chapter of the Full Gospel Business Men's Fellowship International (FGBMFI) in the early '70's, his stirring testimony of God's protection and the empowering of the Holy Spirit, touched many hearts and lives.

But equally impressive was the way in which this hardened combat veteran *physically* touched each person in attendance by saying, *"Come on, be the first one in your neighborhood to hug a Marine Major."* It didn't matter whether he was speaking at a FGBMFI meeting, visiting a neighbor, or working with his fellow officers at the Pentagon, the love of Jesus flowed from this man in a supernaturally, natural way. The last I heard of Merle several years ago, he had been promoted twice, and was now a Colonel. More importantly, he was still receiving promotions in the Army of God.

Scripture is quite clear that there is a heaven, and there is a hell. It is also clear that those who receive Jesus, and truly believe in their heart that His sacrifice on the cross (not their own good works) is what enables them to have eternal life, will in fact, go to heaven.

Taking this a step further, it is also clear that once in heaven, there are different levels of reward, based on what each believer did while on earth (see Mt.16:27, 1 Cor.3:8 and Rev.22:12). We won't speculate here as to what these different levels of reward might be; for 1st Corinthians 2:9 tells us that *"...eye has not seen, and ear has not heard...all that God has prepared for those who love Him."* Furthermore, the Psalmist proclaims, *"...I had rather be a doorkeeper in the house of my God, than to dwell in the tents of wickedness"* (Ps.84:10).

During my two years at Fort Benning, the evidence of a system of rewards in the military was easily seen in the types of housing provided: enlisted men were housed in austere wooden barracks; non-commissioned officers lived in modest homes; officers had nicer quarters, depending on rank; and the base commander lived in a veritable palace. So, whether you want to be a doorkeeper, a member of the choir, a golf pro, or a librarian – whether you want to live in a castle, a bungalow, a split level, or a condo - what are the qualifications required to get you the promotions that will help you reach your heavenly goals? Let's examine a few of them.

**Faithfulness.** In the parable of the talents (Mt.25:14-29), Jesus makes it clear that whether we've been entrusted with a little or with a lot, He expects us to be faithful in making the most of it. We need to ask ourselves, how am I using my time, my money and other resources God has blessed me with? Am I making the best use of the opportunities He gives me to tell others about Him, or to bless them in other ways? Am I being faithful with what He has given me, so that He can trust me with even more? (See verses 21, 23 and 29). Will I someday hear Him say, *'Well done, good and faithful servant'*?"

Faithfulness is part of the fruit of the Spirit (Ga.5:22), and should therefore be evident in the life of every Christian who is growing into the image of Jesus. This includes being faithful in the exercise of the disciplines we learned in Basic Training (see Chapter 3). Revelation 2:10, describes some pretty intense spiritual warfare, that could result in death for some of the soldiers in God's Army. But Jesus makes it clear that those who are *"faithful until death"* will receive a great promotion, *"the crown of life."*

**Spiritual Excellence.** At one time, the US Army used the recruiting slogan, *"Be All That You Can*

*Be.*" It's possible that they got this idea from the Bible. Jesus told his followers to *"...be perfect, even as your Father in heaven is perfect*" (Mt.5:48). The writer of Hebrews tells us to *"...go on unto perfection"* (He.6:1). And Paul says, *"...I press on toward the goal for the prize of the upward call of God in Christ Jesus"* (Phil.3:14).

The word *perfect* as used here does not mean "without fault," it simply means "mature." And spiritual maturity is something that requires some effort on our part, as we yield to the work of the Holy Spirit in our lives. Paul says it well in Philippians 2:12-13 which urges us to "*work out your salvation with fear and trembling; for it is God at work in you both to will and to do for His good pleasure.*" This is *partnering* with God: allowing Him to do His part, and making sure we don't neglect doing our part. An example of this principle occurred in the War of 1812. At the battle of New Orleans, Andrew Jackson urged his troops to *"Trust in the Lord, and keep your powder dry."* Figure 1, below, helps to illustrate this concept.

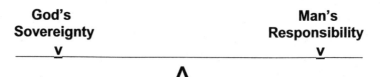

**God's Sovereignty** v — **Man's Responsibility** v

^

**<u>Figure 1</u>** – The Balanced Christian Life is like a sea-saw; If we say I'm not going to do anything until God makes a move or tells me what to do, we get "out of balance"; or if we say everything depends on what I do, we will be "out of balance."

Learning to live the Balanced Christian Life is part of the process of attaining spiritual excellence; and it doesn't happen overnight.

**Perseverance.** Other words that are closely related to perseverance are endurance, steadfastness and patience (longsuffering) , which is also part of the fruit of the Spirit (Ga.5:22). So, overcoming in the face of hardships and trials, quite often results in a *battlefield commission* - a promotion that comes as a result of taking action over and above the call of duty.

Whether it's a hill that needs to be taken, or praying a friend through to victory – whether it's knocking out an enemy target, or loving an unsaved relative into the Kingdom of God – whether it's a secret mission behind enemy lines, or reaching out to someone who is hurting (or perhaps who has hurt you) – perseverance, endurance, steadfastness and patience are qualities that must be part of the arsenal of the soldier in God's Army if he expects to receive promotion.

When difficult situations arise, most of us would prefer to withdraw, retreat, deny reality, or in any way possible avoid conflict or confrontation. Unfortunately, such behavior doesn't make the problem go away. We are called to stand firm. And when we do, some wonderful things happen. James says, "*Blessed is the man who perseveres under trial; for once he has been approved, he will receive the crown of life...*" (Ja.1:12). In describing his own persevering lifestyle, Paul says the promotion he will receive will be a *crown of righteousness* (2 Tim.4:7-8). As we learn to develop perseverance, we earn the right to be called an *OVERCOMER.* And the promise that Jesus holds out to all who are *overcomers,* is to sit with Him on His throne in God's Kingdom (Rev.3:21). Now that's a promotion worth working for.

**Fruitfulness.** Jesus had a lot to say about fruit. He said He expected His followers to *bear fruit that would remain* (Jn.15:16). He said that fruit should be the measuring stick for a prophet (Mt.7:15-20), and also for those claiming to be His followers (Lu.6:43-45). As we stated earlier, the fruit of the Spirit described in Galatians 5:22-23, should be evident to some degree in the life of every Christian.

One of Webster's definitions for fruit is *"the product of any action."* In applying this definition, we might also say that fruit could be the influence we have on the lives of others. Referring to portions of John Chapter 15, author Bruce Wilkinson says, *"For years I read this passage as a general call to Christians to bring others to Christ. But there's no reason to restrict Jesus' meaning of **fruit** to winning souls. I have traced the words **fruit** and **good works** in the Bible, and they're used nearly interchangeably"* [i].

In addressing the elders of the early Church, Peter encouraged them to shepherd the flock in a

Godly manner, being a good example for those under their care, with the promise that when Jesus returns, they would receive another promotion – *the unfading crown of glory* (1Pe.5:1-4). Every soldier in God's Army does well to ask himself if the fruit he is allowing the Holy Spirit to produce in his own life, plus the fruit he is producing by his influence on those around him, will contribute to his qualifications for promotion.

**Obedience.** The Sermon on the Mount (chapters 5, 6 and 7 of Matthew's Gospel) has often been referred to as the constitution and bylaws of the Kingdom of God. Jesus concluded this dynamic message with a memorable word picture. He tells of two men, each of whom built a house – one who built on a rock foundation, and the other who built upon sand. The same storms and floods hit both houses, and we all know that the house built on the rock survived, while the one on sand did not. By telling us that everyone who hears His words and *does them* is like the wise man that built upon the rock, He is stating that the foundation for a successful and prosperous life is *OBEDIENCE* to God.

Throughout scripture we find case after case where God has rewarded the obedience of His people. A few examples follow:

| People Rewarded | Promised Reward | Scripture |
|---|---|---|
| The Israelites | Become God's own treasure | Ex.19:5 |

| People Rewarded | Promised Reward | Scripture |
|---|---|---|
| The Israelites | Things go well for them and their children, forever | Dt. 5:29 |
| Solomon | Have his life lengthened | 1 Kings 3:14 |
| Every believer | Will be blessed in what he does | Ja.1:25 |
| Every believer | Tree of Life; enter Heaven | Rev.22:14 |

Obedience is learned behavior. Hebrews 5:8 tells us that even Jesus *"learned obedience by the things which He suffered."* And 1 John:2:6 makes it clear that those who follow Jesus need to *walk as He walked.* So, there you have it: if you want to qualify for promotion in God's Army, get ready for some obedience training.

~~~~~~~~~~~~~~

As we look at these five qualifications for promotion, it becomes obvious that they are all somehow intertwined. It is also true that most of us have room for improvement in each of these areas. To put it another way, we need to change. We need to grow spiritually.

If you ever have the feeling that you are on a spiritual plateau, it is an illusion: we are either
~~~~~~~~~~~~~~

moving toward God, or away from Him. One of many scriptures that confirms this is Proverbs 4:18 which states, *"...the path of the righteous is like the light of dawn, that shines brighter and brighter until the full day."*

It is true that we are saved by grace on the basis of faith. But James tells us that *faith without works is dead* (Ja.2:17). And so, for every soldier in the Army of God who desires promotion, it becomes mandatory that we change – that we grow spiritually as we develop the qualities of Faithfulness, Spiritual Excellence, Perseverance, Fruitfulness and Obedience. This, of course, is an ongoing process. And with the process well underway, it is now time to identify the enemy.

~~~~~~~~~~
~~~~~~~~~~

## DISCUSSION GUIDE
## FOR CHAPTER FOUR

1. Rate yourself on a scale of 1-5 (5 being very good) on the five qualities needed for promotion:

| Quality | My Score |
|---|---|
| Faithfulness | ________ |
| Spiritual Excellence | ________ |
| Perseverance | ________ |
| Fruitfulness | ________ |
| Obedience | ________ |

2. What rewards (promotions) do you hope to receive? Why?

3. What steps do you need to take that might help improve your chances of promotion?

ENDNOTES

[i] SECRETS OF THE VINE – by Bruce Wilkinson with David Kopp
Copyright © 2001 by Bruce Wilkinson
Publisher: Multnomah Publishers Inc. - PO Box 1720
Sisters, OR 97759

# CHAPTER FIVE

## IDENTIFYING THE ENEMY

*"Now it came about when all the kings who were beyond the Jordan...the Hittite and the Amorite, the Canaanite, the Perizzite, the Hivite and the Jebusite, heard of it, they gathered themselves together with one accord to fight against Joshua and Israel."* Jos.9:1-2

It happened in Korea, and then again to a greater degree in Vietnam. Enemy troops disguised as civilians inflicted numerous casualties on American soldiers; and the inevitable converse, innocent civilians being mistaken for the enemy lost their lives at the hands of well intentioned American GIs. Such incidents dramatize the importance of being able to properly identify the enemy.

In the Preface of this book, it is stated that while much has been written about dealing with Satan and demons, there seems to be a lack of understanding about dealing with our other two spiritual adversaries – *the world* and *the flesh.* This has caused many Christians to become casualties of war, and in some cases to suffer total defeat. The old Flip Wilson phrase, *"The devil made me do it,"* has all too often become the excuse of Christians under attack, when they really have no idea of the origin of their problems. In order to be victorious soldiers in God's Army, we must be able to identify the enemy.

As is obvious, *the world, the flesh* and *the devil* frequently combine forces in their efforts to defeat God's people, in the same way that Israel's enemies formed alliances against them when they entered the Promised Land (see scripture at the beginning of this chapter). To help us with the process of identifying the enemy, we will take a look at each of these adversaries, their characteristics, and the strategies they use in their attacks. In the next chapter we shall examine the weapons we have, that if properly used, will give us victory.

**The World**. To understand what "The World" means, as a spiritual enemy, we must first take a look at what it does NOT mean. Scripture tells us that God so loved *the world* that He gave His only begotten Son. Obviously, *the world* here refers to the people living in the world; and, like God, we are to love those people.

Nor does *the world*, as a spiritual enemy, refer to the natural creation; for Genesis makes it clear that when God created the heavens and the earth, He declared them to be "good". And while Satan is allowed a certain degree of power on the earth (Matthew 4:8-9; Ephesians 2:2), Psalm 24:1 states clearly that *"The earth is the Lord's, and all it contains, the world, and those who dwell in it."*

So, if we are to love the people in the world, and the earth itself has been declared by God to be "good", what does the Bible mean when it says things like *"...friendship with the world is hostility toward God"* (James 4:4), and, *"Do not love the world, nor the things* of *the world"* (1 John 2:15)? [<u>*Note:*</u> *This verse really convicts me when I think of the number of times I have said, "I love ice cream", or "I love pizza", or "I love tennis".]*

And just what did Jesus mean when He prayed for His disciples whom he declared to be *"...in the world"* (John 17:11) , and yet told them that *"... because you are not of the world...the world hates you"* (John 15:19)? If nothing else, we can draw the conclusion from these scriptures that we are to love people, but not things; and that we too are to be in the world, but not of the world. But it goes beyond that.

That Jesus Christ came to proclaim and establish the Kingdom of God is clear throughout scripture. As soldiers in God's Army, we are involved in that same task – proclaiming and establishing the Kingdom of God. In John 18:36, Jesus plainly stated that His Kingdom is not of this world. There is, however, a kingdom which is of this world. Some Bible scholars refer to it as *The World System.* It includes such things as politics and government; education and technology; commerce and materialism; secular humanism and other godless philosophies; even organized religion (note, I did not say the Church).

While all the various facets within this *World System* may have good as well as bad points, the entire complex, which we have now identified as

*The World,* is our spiritual enemy, because it is centered on man, not on God. It is an alternative to the Kingdom of God – a counterfeit of what God wants for His children.

Some time ago, I came across a teaching entitled "*The World Upside Down – The World Right Side Up*". Since I don't know the author, I can't give credit, but here it is:

| The World Upside Down | The World Right Side Up |
| --- | --- |
| Blessed are those whose spirits are high, for they sit on top of the world. | Blessed are the poor in spirit, for theirs is the Kingdom of heaven. |
| Blessed are those who refuse to mourn, for they need no comfort. | Blessed are those who mourn, for they shall be comforted. |
| Blessed are the aggressive, for they shall dominate the earth. | Blessed are the meek, for they shall inherit the earth. |
| Blessed are those who are satisfied with their righteousness, for there are more important things to hunger for. | Blessed are those who hunger and thirst for righteousness, for they shall be filled. |
| Blessed are those who have rights, for they shall obtain justice. | Blessed are the merciful, for they shall obtain mercy. |

| Upside Down (cont.) | Right Side Up (cont.) |
|---|---|
| Blessed are those who are sharp of mind, for they "can't see" God. | Blessed are the pure in heart, for they shall see God. |
| Blessed are those who dictate the peace, for they shall play the role of God. | Blessed are the peace-makers, for they shall be called the children of God. |
| Blessed are those who are admired for being so agreeable, for they sit on top of the world. | Blessed are those who are persecuted for righteousness' sake for theirs is the kingdom of heaven. |
| Blessed are you when men like you, accept you, want you for their leader, and consider themselves fortunate to know you. Rejoice and be flattered, for great is your prestige on earth; for so men have accepted the conformists who were before you. | Blessed are you when men revile and perse-cute you and say all kinds of evil against you falsely for My sake. Rejoice and be glad, for great is your reward in heaven, for so men persecuted the prophets who were before you. |

Over the past several decades, the mores of contemporary American society have changed significantly, making an even greater contrast between the *kingdom of this world* and the *Kingdom of God.* One example is the issue of *legalized abortion,* which scripture teaches is the taking of innocent life, a clear violation of the sixth commandment.

Other examples include:

*Homosexuality* – the Bible calls it *an abomination to God* (Lev. 18:22; Ro. 1:27), while *the world* calls it *an alternative lifestyle*;

*Pornography* – *the world* insists that this vileness be protected as *freedom of speech*;

*Extra-marital sex* - the Bible calls it adultery and fornication, while *the world* says it's *OK as long as it's between consenting partners.*

Another classic example of how the world attacks the Army of God appeared in an article on "growing old" in the June 4, 2001 issue of U.S. NEWS & WORLD REPORT. Here's a quote: "*...senior romances can be legally treacherous. David Cherry, a Boston-based specialist on family law, sometimes warns against marriage so seniors can preserve their assets should their mate get sick.*" Translation: it's OK to commit adultery if there is an economic benefit.

As this chapter is being written, the events of September 11, 2001 are fresh in mind. While we mourn the horrific loss of innocent lives resulting from the terrorist attacks, we can learn some valuable lessons on spiritual warfare with *the World.* Certainly, no disrespect is intended for those who worked in the World Trade Center or the Pentagon; after all, as human beings, we are all in *the World* to one degree or another. But the buildings attacked can easily be seen as symbols of the *World System.* Chapters 17 and 18 of Revelation describe the final outcome of this *World System,* which it refers to as *"Babylon"* and *"The Great Harlot".*

While the language of Revelation is largely symbolic, one can easily see various elements of *the World System* such as politics ( *"kings of the earth"* - 17:2 ), and commerce *("the merchants of the earth"* - 18:11). Of particular interest is the double use of the words *"...is fallen, is fallen..."* in Rev. 18:2, and the total destruction by fire referred to in Rev. 18:8.

The key verse is 17:14 which makes it clear that there is a war between *the Kingdom of God* and the *kingdom of this World,* and the Victor is Jesus (along with all who are found *in Him*). This does not mean that those responsible for the terrorist attacks are a part of the Kingdom of God; on the contrary, God frequently used the enemies of Israel to bring His people to a place of repentance and restoration.

In the following chapters, we shall talk more about our role as soldiers in the battle against *the World.*

**The Flesh.** In chapters seven and eight of Romans,

Paul talks a great deal about the struggle between *the spirit* and *the flesh.* Jesus made the statement that "...*the spirit* is willing, but *the flesh* is weak" (Mt. 26:41). And in Galatians 5:19-23, Paul contrasts the works *the Flesh* with the fruit of *the spirit.* From the context of these passages, it is quite clear that *the flesh* has a deeper meaning than just the soft part of our physical bodies. To better understand why *the flesh* is considered our spiritual enemy, we need to take a look at the nature of man.

In Genesis, we are told that *God created man in His own image.* Many Bible scholars interpret this to mean that since God is a triune being (Father, Son and Holy Spirit), he made man to be a triune being (body, soul and spirit). There are many passages of scripture which refer to these different aspects of man's nature, a principal one being 1 Thes. 5:23 which says, "*...may your spirit, soul and body be preserved complete...*"

This triune nature of man is usually explained along the following lines:

<u>The Body</u> is our **world-consciousness**,

<u>The Soul</u> is our **self-consciousness,**

<u>The Spirit</u> is our **God-consciousness.**

Figure 2 on the next page, helps to clarify this concept.

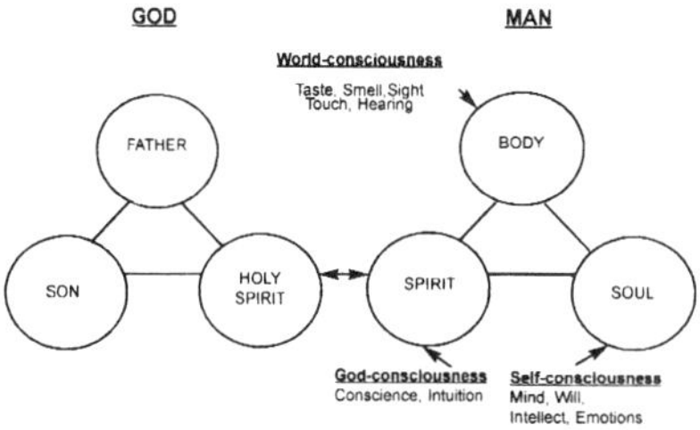


**Figure 2** – Man, created by God as a triune being, communicateswith God in the realm of the Spirit. The spirit is the part of man that died when Adam and Eve sinned, resulting in the need for a spiritual re-birth (Gen. 2:17;Jn. 3:3-8; 1:11-13).

Jether Vinson, one of the finest Bible teachers I ever sat under, used to say that the question of the ages is, *"Who's going to get the body?"*. He was referring, of course, to the issue of whether our body will be controlled by our soul (ie. our own will and emotions), or by our spirit (which for the Christian has been regenerated by the Holy Spirit). Thus, the term *flesh* refers to the body being under the control of the soul of man, rather than his spirit.

In Galations 5: 19-20, Paul lists the works of *the flesh* as *adultery, fornication, lewdness, idolatry, sorcery, hatred, wrath, heresies, selfish ambition, murder, envy, drunkenness and other things like these.* When a person is involved in such activities, there is often a tendency to say the devil is at work in their life. While that may be true, more than likely, the devil may just be standing on the sidelines cheering.

Every day, every soldier in God's Army has choices to make: will I walk in *the spirit*, or in *the flesh?* (Ro. 8:4); Will I set my mind on things of *the spirit*, or of *the flesh*? (Ro.8:5-6); Will I live by *the spirit*, or by *the flesh*? (Ro.8:13).

And if you have any doubts about whether or not this is spiritual warfare, read again the struggle that Paul describes in Romans 7:14-25, where he says such things as, *"...I am not practicing what I would like to do, but am doing the very thing I hate..."* and, *"...I know that nothing good dwells in me, that is in my flesh; for the wishing is present in me, but the doing of the good is not."* Sounds like warfare to me!

**The Devil.** Two common names for this enemy are the Devil (slanderer) and Satan (adversary). But scripture has many other ways of describing this rascal whom we often refer to as "old slewfoot." Here are a few:

Accuser of the brethren (Rev. 12:10)
Adversary (1 Pet. 5:8)
Beelzebub (Mat. 12:24)
Belial (2 Cor. 6:15)
Deceiver of the whole world (Rev. 12:9)
The great dragon (Rev. 12:9)
The evil one (Mat. 13: 19, 38)
The father of lies (Jn. 8:44)
The god of this age (2 Cor. 4:4)
A liar (Jn. 8:44)
Murderer (Jn. 8:44)
The old serpent (Rev. 12:9)

The prince or ruler of this world (Jn. 12:31; 14:30)
Prince of the power of the air ((Eph. 2:2)
The tempter (1 Thes. 3:5)

So, just who is this character, and what makes him an enemy of the Army of God? A common misconception is that the Devil is an independent rival of God, representing the forces of evil in a struggle against God and the forces of good.

While this concept has an element of truth, we need to realize that the devil is NOT *omnipotent* (although he is very powerful); he is NOT *omniscient* (although he is quite shrewd); and he is NOT *omnipresent* (he can only be in one place at a time – which means that when we feel the devil is really after us, it is probably just one of his demons, which we discuss further on in this chapter).

He is a spiritual being who was originally created "good". Proverbs 16:4 states that "*The Lord has made everything for its own purpose, even the wicked for the day of evil.*" There is no clear scriptural reference as to when he was created. It was apparently before the creation of man, since he was present in the form of a serpent in the Garden of Eden. This, incidentally, is where the struggle between mankind and Satan began (Gen. 3:14-15).

My own belief is that angels, including Lucifer (Satan's name before he fell), were created on the first day of creation. That was the day on which

God created light, which He saw as "good", and separated it from darkness (Gen.1:4-5). Since the sun and moon were not created until the fourth day, it stands to reason that the *day and night* (or *light and darkness*) of the first day were spiritual terms, which could have included the creation of spiritual beings, angels.

Two passages of scripture which are often interpreted as a description of the creation and fall of the Devil are Is. 14:12-20 and Ezek. 28:12-19. If such interpretation is correct, we may conclude the following about Satan:

- he was created as a beautiful, anointed cherub to lead God's heavenly host (Ezek. 28:13-14);

- he became proud, and tried to elevate himself to the level of God (Is. 14:13-14; Ezek. 28:17);

- as a result of his pride, he was cast out of heaven (Is. 14:12; Ezek. 28:17; confirmed in Lu. 10:18 and 1 Tim. 3:6);

- his ultimate destination is hell (Is. 14:15; Ezek. 28: 18-19; confirmed in Rev. 20:10).

Before we discuss what makes him an enemy of the Army of God, there are two other very important things we need to know about the devil:

1. he's got an army, too (about a third of the original angelic host according to Rev. 12:3, 4 & 9; Jude 6; and 2 Pe. 2:4) and;

2. Satan and his army (known as demons, evil spirits or fallen angels) are conducting their warfare against God's Army on planet earth.

A logical question to ask at this point is, "if Satan and his demons are fallen, or bad angels, what is the role of the *good* angels in spiritual warfare?" Since the main emphasis of this book is to equip soldiers in God's Army, we will say very little on this question, other than that *good* angels play a very significant part in many spiritual battles.

For those interested in this subject, there are many excellent books available, two of which I will personally recommend. They are: ANGELS, by Billy Graham[i]. This is a scholarly work that deals with questions such as how angels differ from man; how angels are organized; various roles of angels such as protecting us, being messengers of God, and many more. The second book is a novel by Frank Peretti, THIS PRESENT DARKNESS[ii]. Bear in mind, this is fiction, but it is good reading, and it gives a very vivid picture of warfare between *good* and *bad* angels, and their involvement with mankind.

By his nature, Satan is opposed to everything the Kingdom of God stands for. As Jesus put it, *"The thief (Satan) comes only to steal, and kill, and destroy..."* (Jn. 10:10). He and his demons work very hard to keep unregenerated mankind from entering into a relationship with Jesus Christ. And, he is especially antagonistic toward soldiers in the Army of God, as stated by Peter: *"Your adversary, the devil, prowls about like a roaring lion, seeking someone to devour"* (1 Pe. 5:8).

Almost everything the devil or one of his angels will say to you is an absolute lie, or a distortion of the truth. Some of the other strategies he and his army of demons use are as follows:

...they may tempt us (Mt.4:1);

...they may oppose us (Zech. 3:1);

...they may afflict us with disease (Job 2:7);

...they may prompt us to sin (Acts 5:3);

...they may possess and torment us (Mrk. 5:2-5);

...they may divert us from God and His truth (Acts 13:6-12);

...they may cause us to act "religious" (Acts 16:16-18);

...they may pose as angels of light (2 Cor. 11:14);

...they may influence political, geographical and other types of organizations (Eph. 6:12);

...they wage war against the good angels (Dan. 10:10-13).

There are two important pieces of good news to keep in mind when doing battle with the Devil:

*First* - Satan can not do anything to us that God does not allow (Job 1:12; 2:6; Rev. 20:1-3).

And *second* - Jesus has given his disciples (soldiers in God's Army) power and authority over all demons (Lu. 9:1). In the next chapter we will be looking at the weapons He has provided that enable us to exercise that power and authority.

~~~~~~~~~~~

There you have it: three formidable enemies who often combine forces to attempt to defeat the soldier in God's Army. Let's say that before you answered the call of God on your life you were a bank robber. Now *the world* has been telling you that people who really amount to anything drive BMWs and Jaguars, not Chevys and Fords. Your *flesh* has recently manifested envy over the fact that all your neighbors drive better cars than you do. And *the devil* has planted in the mind of a friend of yours (who just happens to be a bank teller), a plan for embezzling $100,000, which he will split with you, provided you help him pull it off. As a former bank
~~~~~~~~~~~

robber, you know the plan can't possibly fail. Most of us were never bank robbers; but we have other types of sinful behavior in our background that *the World, the Flesh and the Devil* can use to attack us. Chapter six will tell us how to use the weapons God has given His soldiers to fight back.

~~~~~~~~~~~

**DISCUSSION GUIDE**
**FOR CHAPTER FIVE**

1. List three ways that *the World* has attacked you and/or someone close to you.

2. List three aspects of your *flesh* that need to be brought more under the control of your spirit.

3. Give one example of how you have been attacked by the *devil.* Explain how you knew it was the *devil,* and not *the world* or your *flesh.*

ENDNOTES

[i] ANGELS: GOD'S SECRET AGENTS by Billy Graham
Copyright © 1975, 1986, 1994
Word Publishing - Dallas, London, Vancouver, Melbourne

[ii] THIS PRESENT DARKNESS by Frank Peretti
Copyright © 1986
Publisher: Crossway Books - Westchester, IL 60153
~~~~~~~~~~~

# CHAPTER SIX

## THE WEAPONS OF OUR WARFARE

*"...for the weapons of our warfare are not of the flesh, but divinely powerful for the destruction of fortresses."* 2 Cor. 10:4

After completing BIOC (Basic Infantry Officers Course) in 1955, I was assigned as an instructor in the Weapons Department of the Infantry School at Fort Benning, GA. Both as a student and an instructor, I learned that each soldier had at least one weapon he was thoroughly trained in. For the members of a Rifle Squad, it was the M-1 Rifle. For most officers, it was a Carbine or a .45 caliber pistol. There were also specialists trained with the BAR (Browning Automatic Rifle).

All instructors in the Weapons Department were required to qualify with the M-1, the Carbine, the .45, and the BAR. It was on these four weapons that we gave various groups of trainees detailed instructions – everything from the nomenclature of various parts, the care and cleaning, correct firing positions, how to develop accuracy, and more.

As students, not only were we taught how to care for and use these weapons, but we were also given instruction on hand-to-hand combat, the use of a bayonet, how to set explosive charges, and the use of hand grenades. In addition, we viewed demonstrations of various other weapons, ranging from bazookas and recoilless rifles, to machine guns and heavy artillery.

Modern military weapons are, of course, much more sophisticated than the arsenal of fifty-plus years ago. The point is that the men and women of our armed forces have always had a variety of weapons to use in fighting the battles against the enemies of our nation.

And so it is with the soldiers in God's Army. We too have a great assortment of weapons at our disposal for doing battle with *the world, the flesh* and *the devil.* And if we are to be victorious, it is essential for each of us to be well equipped and thoroughly trained in the use of our spiritual weapons.

Before we get into a detailed list of our spiritual weapons, we need to examine a few general characteristics common to all of them, as seen in 2 Corinthians 10:3-5. To begin with, they are *spiritual* weapons – that is, they are not of the flesh. Secondly, they are *divinely powerful,* or as the King James version says, they are *mighty in God.* And third, their purpose is for the *destruction of fortresses,* which the King James version calls *strongholds.* Fortresses or strongholds are the domain of all three of our spiritual enemies. Here are some examples:

| Enemy | Fortress/Stronghold |
| --- | --- |
| The World | 1 Cor. 1:18-28 explains how God deals with the things this world considers to be wise and powerful. This could include the institutions of government, education, organized religion commerce, etc. |
| The Flesh | 2 Cor.10:5 lists imaginations, speculations and ungodly thoughts – all of these are controlled by our mind, which is a key element of our flesh. Another example might be strong emotions such as anger, jealousy, etc. |
| The Devil | Mt. 12:26 and Lu. 11:18 are but two of the scriptures that make it clear that Satan has a kingdom. But as stated in the previous chapter, the fall of his kingdom is just a matter of time. |

## Our Spiritual Arsenal

The Bible lists many spiritual weapons. Here are some of the most important ones, along with some ideas on which enemies they are most effective against, and how to become proficient in their use.

**Scripture**. Ephesians 6:17 refers to the word of God as *"the sword of the Spirit"*, and Hebrews 4:12 says it is *"sharper than any two edged sword."* At the beginning of His ministry, Jesus was confronted in the wilderness by Satan, who used scripture (out of context) to try to tempt the Lord. Jesus used His "sword" (scripture in proper context) to send Satan on his way. A modern day example of using scripture as a spiritual weapon is the ministry of Prison Fellowship. Founded by convicted Watergate conspirator, Chuck Colson, PF has taken the Word of God into hundreds of prisons worldwide, through Bible studies, one-on-one counseling, drama and music. The result has been that thousands of prisoners have been delivered from their spiritual enemies (*the world, the flesh and the devil*).

When tempted by the lusts of *the flesh*, the lies of *the devil*, or the allures of *this world*, every soldier in God's army needs to be ready to speak with authority an appropriate portion of God's word to combat the enemy attack. Some guidelines on how to become proficient in using this weapon are found in Chapter 3, Basic Training.

**The Blood Of The Lamb**. In chapter 12 of Revelation, we have a picture of spiritual warfare in heaven (verses 7 & 8), and on earth (verses 9-11). One of the weapons used here by the soldiers in God's army to overcome the devil (the dragon and his angels) is *"the blood of the Lamb."* This weapon, along with *"the word of their testimony"* (see below), are effectively used together to gain the victory. This combination can be especially effective in thwarting any satanic attack.

In His last public discourse, knowing that He would soon be shedding His blood on the cross, Jesus said, *"...now, the ruler of this world shall be cast out."* An often quoted bit of advice is that when Satan reminds you of your past, just remind him of his future. It's okay to speak to the devil or an evil spirit (after all, Jesus did), but be careful not to assume the same attitude as when you are in prayer. In other words, avoid the appearance of praying to the devil.

When under satanic attack, say something like, *"Satan, you and all your host are defeated by the blood of the Lamb, and I'm God's child, washed in His blood, so I command you to take your hands off me."* This is an excellent way to use this weapon.

Another way is to apply *the blood of the Lamb* over loved ones, or others you pray for (such as spiritual and governmental leaders) who might be subject to demonic attack. A prayer that asks God to cover a person with *the blood of the Lamb* to protect them from enemy attack, and to give them grace to live a testimony that is pleasing to the Father, can and should be used on a daily basis.

The term "*plead the Blood*" is one I've often heard used, but I'm not sure of its scriptural basis. We don't have to plead for the blood of the Lamb; it has already been shed for us, and is freely available to us today.

**The Word of Our Testimony.** This is the other half of the knockout punch referred to in Revelation 12:11. Since Satan and all of his angels are liars, one of their chief tactics is to heap condemnation upon soldiers in God's Army by reminding them of all the rotten things they have done, said or thought. This is why he is referred to as "*the accuser of the brethren.*" When this happens, we of course need to be sure there is no sin in our life that has not been confessed and repented of.

With that done, we can then boldly tell any demonic spirit who we are in Christ; and that what He has done for us by dying on the cross to pay the penalty for our sins, has made us righteous before our God. Our testimony should focus on what He has done and how it has affected us. This should be in your own words, relating to your personal experience with God.

It's always good, however, to reinforce your testimony with scripture. For example: In Christ, I am accepted (according to John 1:12, *I am His child*); In Christ, I am secure (according to Romans 8:31-39, *nothing can separate me from His love*); In Christ, I am significant (according to John 15:16, *He has chosen and appointed me to bear fruit).*

God's Word is full of expressions that describe the way He has changed the lives of His children.

Using His Word brings glory to Him, rather than to us. He deserves the Glory. We do not.

Many *lay people* feel that preaching should be left to the clergy. Yet, there is something powerful about a sincere testimony that gives glory to God. The late Demos Shakarian, founder of the Full Gospel Business Men's Fellowship International, in describing the events that led up to the start of FGBMFI, wrote the following: *"I thought of other things: the dining room at Knotts Berry Farm when the face of one man after another seemed to light up with the glory of God – the impact of listening to these men describe their experiences. What an irresistible force it could be if hundreds – thousands – of such men would band together to spread this kind of good news all over the world..."* [i] And so they did!! FGBMFI has had its ups and downs, but there is no denying the thousands of lives that have been changed for the good as a result of hearing an "untrained" layman give glory to God for what He has done in his life.

In one sense, every word that we speak is a part of our testimony. That's why as soldiers in God's Army we should avoid using negative words – words that criticize or tear down. Grumbling, gossip, complaining, and other negative speech patterns play right into the hands of *the devil.*

When we fail to choose our words carefully, we are usually helping our enemy, rather than fighting him. James 3:1-12 offers some sound advice on how to have a good testimony. *"If anyone is never at fault in what he says, he is a perfect (mature) man, able to keep his whole body in check"* (James 3:2). Most of us are not "perfect" or all that mature; nevertheless, that should be our goal.

**The Mind of Christ**. It has often been said that the mind is a battlefield. Most of us can bear witness to that. Paul describes some of the battles that took place in his mind in Romans 7:18-25. Yet it was this same Paul who said, *"...we have (not some day may have) the mind of Christ"* (1.Cor. 2:16). In Romans 8:5-6, Paul speaks further about what it means to have the mind of Christ, when he says, *"Those who live according to the flesh set their minds on things of the flesh, but those who live according to the Spirit, the things of the Spirit. For to be carnally minded is death, but to be spiritually minded is life and peace."*

It is clear that this is a battle between the soldier in God's Army and his old nemisis, *the flesh.* (We talked about that battle in Chapter 5). It would seem, therefore, that when Paul says we have the mind of Christ, he means it is available for us to use as a spiritual weapon whenever we choose to.

So, how do we go about making use of this weapon more frequently, rather than relying on our old fleshly mind? The answer lies in a process called *renewal of the mind.* In Romans 12:2, Paul says, *"...do not be conformed to* ***this world****, but be transformed by the renewing of your mind."* (Notice, we now have a second spiritual enemy, *the world,* against which we can use this weapon).

The first thing I think of when the subject of *mind renewal* comes up is the old computer acronym, GIGO (Garbage In – Garbage Out.) Most of us spend far too much time watching TV shows and other forms of entertainment that put the wrong kinds of thoughts into our minds. The result is that those *wrong thoughts* often result in *wrong behavior.* Restricting our exposure to *worldly* influences is especially important prior to going to bed at night. I used to watch Jay Leno, or The Tonight Show, or MASH before going to bed. While these may seem to be a harmless means of inducing sleep, I found they were having a negative impact on my dreams and subsequent thought patterns. I now usually spend those last waking moments of each day reading a Christian book or other devotional literature. Some soldiers in God's Army prefer to spend that time in prayer or reading scripture.

We probably can't prevent carnal or worldly thoughts from entering our mind, but we can prevent them from staying there. When they come in, we need to *"nip 'em in the bud."* The best way to do this is by following Paul's advice in Philippians 4:8, where he tells us to let our minds dwell on things that are *true, noble, just, pure, lovely, of good report, virtuous and praiseworthy.* Focusing on these kinds of thoughts will help equip the soldier in God's Army with *the mind of Christ.*

**Armor**. Other than *the sword of the Spirit* (which we covered above under the topic of *Scripture*), the various pieces of armor mentioned in Ephesians 6:13-17 are used primarily for defense, rather than as offensive weapons. These include the girdle of *truth*; the breastplate of *righteousness*; foot coverings of *the preparation of the gospel of peace*; the helmet of *salvation*; and the shield of *faith*. (I love *the shield of faith*, because Ps. 3:3 tells us that *the Lord himself is our shield.)*

Paul says that putting on the full armor of God will enable us to stand firm against the schemes of *the devil* (Eph. 6:11). It should be noted, however, that these pieces of armor can be used in fighting our other spiritual enemies as well. For example, when Jesus said, "*...the truth shall set you free*" (Jn. 8:32-34) He was speaking of freedom from sin, or *the flesh*. And 1 John 5:4 tells us that our *faith* gives us victory that has overcome *the world*. Scripture has a great deal more to say about the qualities represented by these pieces of armor. At this point, however, we will simply say that the soldier in God's Army needs to put on the full armor of God every day.

**Praise and Worship**. In chapter three, we defined praise and worship, and went into detail as to why this should be a regular daily activity for every soldier in God's Army. Now, let's examine how they are used as a spiritual weapon.

In 2 Chronicles 20:22, we read that "*...when they*

*(God's Army) began to sing and to praise, the Lord set ambushes against the people of Ammon, Moab and Mount Seir, who had come against Judah, and they were defeated."* In the New Testament, you may recall the story of Paul and Silas who were imprisoned while spreading the Gospel in Philippi. At midnight, they began to praise and worship the Lord. This resulted in a great earthquake, which loosened everyone's chains and blasted open the prison doors, setting all the prisoners free (Acts 16:24-26).

These are but two of many examples in scripture of how praise and worship release the power of God to do battle for us against our enemies. Further evidence of this is seen in Judges 1:1-4. Here we find the Israelites asking God which tribe should lead the way into battle against the Canaanites. The Lord tells them to *send Judah first.* It's no coincidence that the name Judah means *praise*.

King David was not only a great warrior, but a great man of praise and worship. It is not surprising therefore, that several of his Psalms make the connection between praise & worship and victory in battle. Some examples are Psalm 68:1-4, and Psalm 149:6-9.

In his book SILENCING THE ENEMY[ii], songwriter Robert Gay says: "*Every move of God has produced new songs and choruses that declare what is being preached and taught. We are in the midst of a prophetic move of God, He is bringing forth in this hour a great company of prophets and prophetic songwriters. The trumpet is sounding, and the troops are assembling as they hear the word of the Lord. Spiritual warfare is one of those messages."*

When under attack by any of our spiritual enemies, praise and worship should be among the first weapons used by every soldier in God's Army.

**Prayer and Fasting.** As with Praise & Worship, we dealt with prayer in chapter three, pointing out that this discipline needs to be a regular part of the daily experience of every soldier in the Army of God. Nothing was mentioned there, however, about fasting, primarily because it is not something most Christians do every day.

When Jesus taught about fasting, however, He said, *"...**when** you fast"*, NOT *"...**if** you fast"* (Mt. 6:16-18). In this teaching from the sermon on the mount, He also made it clear that our fasting should be done with right motives, and never done to call attention to ourselves. Another excellent teaching on fasting is found in Isaiah 58:3-12. This passage contrasts fasting that is done with wrong motives, as opposed to fasting that pleases God. Using terminology like *"...share your bread with the hungry"* (vs. 7), we definitely get the idea that this is a weapon designed to deal with our *flesh.* And the promise, *"Then you shall call and the Lord will answer..."* (vs. 9) helps us see the effectiveness of fasting as a spiritual weapon.

Mark 9:17-29 tells the story of a man who brought his son, a deaf mute with an evil spirit, to Jesus for healing and deliverance. He had previously brought his son to Jesus' disciples, but they were unable to help the boy. After Jesus set the boy free, His disciples asked Him how He was able to do it, while they were not. The Lord's well-known answer was, *"This kind comes out by nothing but prayer and fasting."* Two things we learn from this incident are that prayer and fasting usually work together as a spiritual weapon; and that fasting can be used to combat not only our *flesh*, but also *the devil (and all his angels).*

The November 26, 2001 issue of U.S. NEWS & WORLD REPORT carried an article about the escape from Afghanistan of eight foreign aid workers (including two Americans) who had been arrested for "preaching Christianity." During the more than 3 months they were held captive, many soldiers in God's Army around the world prayed and fasted on behalf of those brothers and sisters in Christ. Their exciting and dramatic rescue gives clear evidence as to the effectiveness of prayer and fasting as spiritual weapons.

**The Name of The Lord**. Invoking the name of Jesus Christ has tremendous power as a spiritual weapon. Whether your mind is being bombarded with impure thoughts, or there is an unmistakable presence of a demonic spirit, or you find your Biblical beliefs in conflict with some "worldly wisdom" - just calling out, "JESUS!" will often deal an immediate blow against the enemy attack. This is not to say that the attack will be over, but it gives the soldier in God's Army a chance to regroup, and determine what weapon to use next. And, many times, it is all that is needed.

David certainly understood this when he confronted Goliath. He said, "*You come to me with a sword, a spear and a javelin. But I come to you* ***in the Name of the Lord of Hosts***" (1 Sam.17:45). We all know who won that battle.

Jesus said, "*...these signs shall follow those who believe:* ***In My Name*** *they will cast out demons..*" (Mk. 16:17). He also gave His disciples (and that includes every soldier in the Army of God, today) authority over all the power of the enemy (Lu. 10:19). And that is why using His Name in spiritual warfare works - because His Name carries with it the authority (or power) of God.

Peter and John knew this when they said to the man lame since birth, "***In the name of Jesus Christ of Nazareth****, rise up and walk.*" And he did! (Acts 3:1-8). Paul also knew it when he cast a spirit of divination out of a slave girl ***in the name of Jesus Christ*** (Acts 16:16-18).

The bottom line is that God has given to Jesus "*...the name which is above every name, that at the name of Jesus every knee shall bow... and every tongue confess that Jesus Christ is Lord to the glory* *of God the Father"* (Phil. 2:9-11). Now that's a weapon that can't be beat.

~~~~~~~~~~

To summarize, we have discussed eight of the weapons that are available to us for spiritual warfare:

**\*Scripture** **\*The Blood of The Lamb**
**\*The Word of Our Testimony** **\*Armor**
**\*Praise & Worship** **\*The Mind of Christ**
**\*Prayer & Fasting** **\*The Name of The Lord**

A few points to keep in mind: Each of these weapons may be especially effective against one particular enemy; By the same token, each can be used against all three of our enemies under certain circumstances; And finally, there may be some battles in which the soldier in God's Army may need to use some combination of the eight weapons almost simultaneously. We'll talk more about that in chapter eight, The Battle Itself.

~~~~~~~~~~

## DISCUSSION GUIDE FOR CHAPTER SIX

1. Which of the eight weapons have you actually used in spiritual warfare?

2. Which of these eight weapons do you feel the most comfortable with?

3. Which are you least comfortable with?

4. What steps do you believe God wants you to take to become fully qualified with the weapons you have not been using?

ENDNOTES

---

[i] THE HAPPIEST PEOPLE ON EARTH – by Demos Shakarian and John & Elizabeth Sherrill
Copyright © 1975 – Published by Chosen Books, Lincoln, VA 22078
Distributed by Word Books, Waco, TX 76703

[ii] SILENCING THE ENEMY by Robert Gay
Copyright © 1993
Publisher: Creation House - 600 Rinehart Rd., Lake Mary, FL 32746

# CHAPTER SEVEN

## PREPARING FOR BATTLE

*"What king, going to make war against another king, does not sit down first and consider whether he is able with ten thousand to meet him who comes against him with twenty thousand?"* (Luke 14:31).

"Be Prepared" is more than the Boy Scouts' motto. It is also sound advice for engaging in spiritual warfare. To do so without a battle plan is like going on a long trip without consulting a map. Putting into practice what we learned in basic training, along with the knowledge gained to help us identify the enemy, will be a part of our plan. We will also need to be sure we are ready to use any and all of the weapons in our spiritual arsenal.

In the scripture quoted above, it is obvious that Jesus endorsed the idea of preparing for battle before launching any kind of attack. In their second attempt to take the city of Ai (we'll talk about the first attempt later on), Joshua spelled out for the Army of Israel the plan that the Lord had given him, which included dividing his troops and setting an ambush. The result was an overwhelming victory (Josh. 8:1-8).

In Jeremiah's description of the destruction of Babylon, he outlines a multi-pronged strategy for obtaining victory:
*1) Sharpen the arrows, fill the quivers;*
*2) Lift up a standard against the walls of Babylon;*

*3) Post a strong guard;*
*4) Station sentries; and*
*5) Place an ambush* (Jer. 51:11-12).

Every battle is different. Thus, our preparation may vary from one situation to another. There are, however, some guiding principles that will help us in developing a plan. Among these are the following: Seek God; Seek Wise Counsel; Check Your Attitude; Remove Any Idols; and Use All Resources. Let's briefly examine each of these.

**Seek God.** *The battle is the Lord's.* David understood and proclaimed this truth when he engaged the giant Goliath, slaying the Philistine champion, and giving Israel a great victory (1 Sam. 17:45-52, esp. vs. 47). Jahaziel, a Levitical prophet, used almost the same words, *"...the battle is not yours, but God's"* (2 Chron. 20:15) as he encouraged King Jehoshaphat when a multi-national army came to wage war against Judah. Nearly all the kings, priests and prophets in the Old Testament understood this principle, and therefore made it a point to seek God before engaging in battle (most of the time).

There was one notable exception when God's people did **not** seek Him before going to war: the first battle of Ai (see Josh. 7:1-12). Following the Lord's directions, Joshua and the Army of Israel, easily conquered and destroyed the city of Jericho. Having done so, they assumed that a much smaller force would be sufficient to give them victory over the little city of Ai. They did not consult the Lord about this. The result: *they got their butts kicked.* When Joshua complained to God about this, he was informed that the reason for the defeat was that there was sin in the camp that needed to be dealt with – something the Lord obviously would have revealed had they first consulted Him.

Many modern day military leaders understand and follow this principle as well. It was heartening to see that U.S. Commander-in-chief, President George W. Bush, called the nation to a day of prayer, and committed himself to prayer, before launching the war on terrorism that was precipitated by the September 11, 2001 attacks on our country.

**Seek Wise Counsel.** Many times God will speak to us through the wisdom of others. Proverbs 20:18 says, *"Plans are established by counsel; by wise counsel wage war."* The book of Proverbs contains several other exhortations to seek wise counsel (though not necessarily pertaining to warfare). The key issue is to determine whether or not the counsel we receive is, in fact, *wise.*

In Exodus 18:19-24, we are told that Moses followed the wise counsel of his father-in-law, Jethro. The results were good. In Daniel 4:27, Daniel gives wise counsel to King Nebuchadnezzar, after interpreting the King's dream. Refusing to accept Daniel's advice, the King went through a rough time that he could have avoided.

The simple truth in all of this is that we need each other. Ted Haggard, author and senior pastor of the 7,000-member New Life Church in Colorado Springs, says, *"God has given us natural relationships that reflect His three-in-one dynamic. Marriage, our families, the church, a community, friendships and alliances – all are opportunities for us to relate to and strengthen one another. People are weak when they don't know how to connect with others. But with connection, great tasks can be accomplished."*[i]

There are soldiers in God's Army who have had experience in casting out demons, praying for the sick, counseling the troubled, and other forms of spiritual warfare. Many times in the past, when I have been called upon to enter into spiritual warfare on behalf of others, I would make a point of seeking the help of others who were knowledgeable and experienced in dealing with such matters.

Whether battling *the world, the flesh,* or *the devil,* using a team approach (assuming you have the right people on your team) may not always guarantee victory, but it offers a much better chance of success in dealing with the problem.

One such case occurred around 1970. Tim, a young man in our home prayer group, called saying that he was having some serious flashbacks, resulting from his previous drug problem. My wife, Betty, and I went to Tim's house, and proceeded to pray and take authority over the evil spirits that were attacking his mind and body. Tim was set free.

On another occasion, Betty and I were praying for a woman who was seeking a healing. Some, but not all sickness can be caused by evil spirits. In this case, the Holy Spirit prompted Betty to ask the woman if there was anyone in her life that she had not forgiven. The flow of bitterness, anger and hatred that came forth from her mouth, directed against her ex husband, was astounding. Further ministry revealed that there was no evil spirit involved, but simply her unwillingness to forgive, that was causing her physical problems. There was no victory that day, nor could there be until the woman was ready to deal with the real enemy, *her flesh*, by confessing the sin of unforgiveness.

A trap that many Christians fall into is that of seeking counsel until we hear what we want to hear. That's what happened in the case of Solomon's son, King Rehoboam. When he was asked to lighten the workload of the children of Israel, he sought advice from some of the elders who had served with his father. But he also sought counsel from some of his contemporaries. He rejected the advice of the elders, which was to *lighten the workload*; and heeded the counsel of the younger men, which was to *be a tough taskmaster*. This resulted in splitting the nation into two groups, Israel and Judah. You can read all about it in 1 Kings, chapter 12.

When we receive conflicting counsel, the other principles discussed below, can be helpful in choosing the right course – Check Your Attitude, Remove Any Idols, and Use All Resources.

**Check Your Attitude.** Sometimes there can be a fine line between being a *wimp* and a *warlord.* The *wimp* somehow feels that he was put on the face of the earth to be a victim of *the world system,* to be kicked around by *the devil,* and to be totally controlled by the desires of *the flesh.* He is ignorant of, or refuses to heed scriptures such as these:

> *"Out of the mouths of babes and nursing infants You have ordained strength (or Praise), because of Your enemies. That You may silence the enemy and the avenger"* (Ps. 8:2).

> *"Let the high praises of God be in their mouth, and a two-edged sword in their hand, to execute vengeance on the nations, and punishment on the peoples; to bind their kings with chains and their nobles with fetters of iron; to execute on them the written judgement – this honor have all His saints"* (Ps. 149:6-9; must be understood as spiritual warfare, not human military conflict.)

> *"Yet, in all these things we are more than conquerors through Him who loved us" (Ro. 8:37).*

*"Behold, I give you power to tread on serpents and scorpions, and over all the power of the enemy..."* (Lu. 10:19).

*"...reckon yourselves to be dead indeed to sin, but alive to God in Christ Jesus our Lord"* (Ro. 6:11).

*"They (Jesus' followers) are not of the world, just as I (Jesus) am not of the world"* (John 17:16).

Whereas the *wimp* does not rightly apply these scriptures in his own life, the *warlord* on the other hand, is apt to apply them in his own strength and intellect with an attitude of pride. This can be equally as dangerous. And neither attitude is befitting a soldier in the Army of God.

A proper attitude includes humility, total dependence upon God, confidence in the finished work of the Cross, while relying on the giftings He has provided. Paul said it well when he wrote, *"Work out your own salvation with fear and trembling, for it is God who works in you both to will and to do for His good pleasure"* (Phil. 2:12-13).

**Remove Any Idols.** *"Then Samuel spoke to all the house of Israel, saying, 'If you return to the Lord with all your heart, remove the foreign gods and Ashtaroth from among you, and direct your hearts to the Lord, and serve Him alone, He will deliver you from the hand of the Philistines'"* (1 Sam. 7:3).

Idols were a major problem with God's people during the periods of the judges and the kings of Israel. And idol worship frequently resulted in defeat at the hands of their enemies. But idols were fairly easy to identify in those days. They were carvings or statues made of wood, stone, metal or some other substance.

Today, however, idols are a little harder to recognize. If we define an idol as anything we put in the place of God, then we can likely build quite a list, many of which may be considered as "good." Let's look at some of our "good" idols, and see what Jesus had to say about them:

> **Family** – Everyone knows that family relationships are important. And God's word gives us lots of wise counsel on how to make and keep our families strong. But all too often, there may be a spouse or child or other family member that we put ahead of God. Jesus says, *"He who loves father or mother more than Me is not worthy of Me, and he who loves son or daughter more than Me is not worthy of Me"* (Mt. 10:37). He's talking about a subtle form of idol worship.
>
> **Religion** – Jesus was more critical of the religious leaders of His day than of anyone else (just read chapters 15, 16 and 23 of Matthew's gospel). One of His most stinging rebukes of "religious" people is found in John 5:39-40, where He says, *"You search the*

*scriptures because you think that in them you have eternal life; and it is these that bear witness of Me; and yet you are unwilling to come to Me, that you may have life."* It is sad to say that numerous churches today include many people who are good at observing religious rules and traditions, but have no real intimate fellowship or communion with God. In these cases, the church and/or our religion has become an idol.

**Good Works** – Now wait a minute you may say – aren't we supposed to do good works? The answer obviously is YES. Paul wrote, *"For we are His workmanship, created in Christ Jesus for good works, which God prepared beforehand, that we should walk in them"* (Eph. 2:10). But when our works become a source of spiritual pride, or a means of creating our own self-righteousness, once again, we have created an idol.

Jesus' parable of the Pharisee and the publican (Luke 18:9-14) is a good example. And Paul writes, *"For not knowing about God's righteousness, and seeking to establish their own, they did not subject themselves to the righteousness of God"* (Ro. 10:3).

Furthermore, Isaiah saw good works as an idol when he wrote, *"...all our righteousness is as filthy rags"* (Is. 64:6).

**Money and Possessions** – Well, everybody knows that *money is the root of all evil*, right? Not really; the Bible says, *"the love of money is a root of all sorts* of evil" (1 Tim. 6:10). The age-old question, *"can a Christian own a Cadillac?"* is best answered, *"Yes, as long as the Cadillac doesn't own him."* In short, money and possessions, in and of themselves, are neither bad nor good. They are neutral.

It is our attitude about them which causes the risk of making them idols. Jesus said, *"No man can serve two masters. Either he will hate the one and love the other, or he will be devoted to the one and despise the other. You cannot serve both God and money"* (Mt. 6:24).

We've listed only four modern day idols, but there are more. Hobbies, job or occupation, habits, activities, relationships, entertainment – all these have the potential for being pleasing to God. But they also have the potential for becoming more important than our relationship with Him. That is when they become idols.

The occult, New Age philosophies and other false religions which deny the uniqueness and divinity of Jesus, can also be classified as modern day idols.

Forsaking our idols may be difficult, but we can take encouragement from Paul's instructions to Timothy, *"Endure hardship with us like a good soldier of Christ Jesus. No one serving as a soldier gets involved in civilian affairs – he wants to please his commanding officer"* (2 Tim. 2:3-4).

**Use All Resources.** In the parable of the five wise and five foolish virgins (Mt. 25:1-13), Jesus explains that the wise virgins were those who took steps to secure a supply of oil for their lamps. The foolish virgins did not. The wise virgins were rewarded by being allowed to attend the wedding. The foolish virgins were left in the dark, indicating that they had no real personal relationship with the Lord.

My understanding of this parable is that the resource which the wise virgins had and the foolish ones lacked, namely OIL, is a type of the Holy Spirit. In the Old Testament, oil was used to anoint both kings and priests (Ex. 29:7; 1 Sam. 10:1), symbolic of the present day anointing of the Holy Spirit on believers (2 Cor. 1:21-22; 1 Jn. 2:20,27). Furthermore, oil is seen symbolically in scripture as producing joy (Ps. 45:7; Is. 61:3), unity of believers (Ps. 133) and healing (Lu. 10:34), all of which are ministries of the Holy Spirit.

If my interpretation of this parable is correct, it stands to reason that every soldier in God's Army would be wise to make certain that he has all of this valuable resource (the oil of the Holy Spirit) that he can obtain. Different denominations and groups within the Body of Christ hold varying views on the fullness of the Holy Spirit.

Since it is not the intent of this book to raise doctrinal issues which may divide Christians, we offer the following quote from a publication of Campus Crusade For Christ, a non-denominational Christian organization:

> "One becomes a Christian through the ministry of the Holy Spirit, according to John 3:1-8. From the moment of spiritual birth, the Christian is indwelt by the Holy Spirit at all times (Jn. 1:12; Col.2:9-10; Jn. 14:16-17). **Though all Christians are indwelt by the Holy Spirit, not all Christians are filled (controlled and empowered) by the Holy Spirit."** [ii]

Pentecostal and Charismatic Christians refer to the experience of being filled with the Holy Spirit as *The Baptism With (or In) the Holy Spirit*, based on scriptures such as John 1:33, Acts 1:4-8; 2:1-4, and others. Other believers may refer to this experience simply as "*being filled with the Spirit.*" Still others may call it something else. And there may even be some who deny the existence or need for such an experience.

Nevertheless, the soldier in God's Army who walks in the *fullness of the Spirit* has at least two things working for him: (1) he has received *power* to live a life that glorifies Christ; and (2) he is more likely to have the spiritual gifts listed in 1 Cor. 12:8-10, working in his life. All these gifts are important, but *the discerning of spirits* can be especially helpful when engaged in spiritual warfare.

If you feel that you don't have all the "OIL" you need, right now would be a good time to ask the Lord to lead you to a mature Christian (one whom you consider to be filled with the Holy Spirit) who can help you take the next step in appropriating all the resources required for spiritual warfare.

To summarize, these five principles should be considered when developing our battle plan:

- Seek God
- Seek wise counsel
- Check your attitude
- Remove all idols
- Use all resources.

~~~~~~~~~~~
~~~~~~~~~~~

## DISCUSSION GUIDE
## FOR CHAPTER SEVEN

Before getting into the battle itself (next chapter) let's do a final checklist to be sure we are ready.

[ ] I know I've been called to active duty as a Soldier in The Army of God

[ ] I've put on the uniform of a soldier in God's Army

[ ] I've completed Basic Training

[ ] I'm working on my qualifications for promotion

[ ] I can identify the enemy: *The World, The Flesh,* and *The Devil*

[ ] I am equipped with all the weapons I'll need

[ ] My battle plan includes:
- Seeking God;
- Seeking the counsel of others;
- The right attitude (neither *wimp* nor *warlord);*
- Removal of idols; and
- Use of all resources.

ENDNOTES

---

[i] THE LIFE GIVING CHURCH by Ted Haggard
Copyright © 1998, 2001, Ted Haggard
Published by Regal Books – a division of Gospel Light, Ventura, CA

[ii] HAVE YOU MADE THE WONDERFUL DISCOVERY OF THE SPIRIT-FILLED LIFE?
Copyright © Campus Crusade For Christ, Inc. – 1966

# CHAPTER EIGHT

## THE BATTLE ITSELF

*"Then it happened in the spring, at the time when kings go out to battle..."* 2 Sam. 11: 1
*"There is an appointed time for everything...a time for war and a time for peace."* Eccl. 3:1, 8

Sooner or later, we will find ourselves involved in a spiritual battle. When this happens, the first thing we must do is determine which of our enemies we are fighting: *the world, the flesh,* or *the devil.* Or is it some combination of the three? Let's look at some of the strategies we should use when engaged in warfare with each of these.

**The Flesh.** In the scripture quoted above, from 2nd Samuel, it is interesting to note when reading further in that chapter, that King David chose to remain in Jerusalem, sending his military leaders off to war. This, however, did not exempt David from a battle of another kind – that with *his flesh.* We are all aware of what ensued – his adulterous affair with Bathsheba, and his subsequent role in the murder of her husband, Uriah.

But the story doesn't end there. Who of us has not at one time or another yielded to the lusts of *the flesh*? Perhaps not adultery or murder, but how about gluttony or too much to drink. Or maybe you're a smoker, and just can't give up that habit because your flesh really craves it. When you are in a battle with *the flesh,* it is important to remember that you can't cast out flesh. Furthermore, rebuking *the flesh* will do little or no good. The first strategy we should employ in a battle with *the flesh* is to **stand against it**.

In Galatians 5:1, Paul reminds us that Christ has set us free from bondage to *the flesh*, when he says, *"Stand firm then, and do not let yourselves be burdened again by a yoke of slavery."* The way we *stand firm* is to use the spiritual weapons we have (see chapter 6), especially *Scripture* and *The Mind of Christ*. When Jesus said, *"The spirit is willing, but the flesh is weak"* (Mt. 26:41), He clearly meant that our *flesh* has a hard time resisting temptation. Said another way, *the flesh* is quite strong when it comes to doing what pleases ourselves.

So what happens when I blow it? - something that every soldier in God's Army will eventually do. This brings us to our second key strategy in dealing with *the flesh* – **repentance.** Chapter 12 of 2nd Samuel tells how David was confronted with his sin, and how he reacted to it. His repentance involved confessing his sin and humbling himself before God with prayer and fasting.

Listen to some of David's thoughts as he cried out to God while reflecting on his moral failure. *"For I acknowledge my transgressions, and my sin is always before me. Against You, You only have I sinned and done this evil in Your sight. Create in me a clean heart, O God, and renew a steadfast spirit within me. Restore to me the joy of Your salvation.*

*The sacrifices of God are a broken spirit, a broken and contrite heart...*" (Ps. 51:3, 4, 10, 12, 17). For David to say that his only sin was against God seems to ignore what he did to Bathsheba and Uriah. But he obviously recognized that true repentance comes only when we realize how much our sin hurts God. This is what Paul was referring to when he wrote, *"For Godly sorrow produces repentance leading to salvation, not to be regretted; but the sorrow of the world produces death"* (2 Cor. 7:10).

So, were a *spirit of lust* and a *spirit of murder* at work in David, causing him to sin? It's possible, but scripture does not say that. If that had been the case, the solution would have been to cast out the evil spirits. David's acts of repentance, however, gave him the victory (in spite of the temporary set-back). And the good news for every soldier in God's Army is that when we sin, *"we have an Advocate with the Father, Jesus Christ the righteous"* (1 Jn.2:1) and, *"If we confess our sins, He is faithful and just to forgive us our sins and to cleanse us from all unrighteousness"* (1 Jn. 1:9).

**The World.** Because we live in *the world* , we are confronted with this enemy every day of our lives. Sometimes it comes against us with a frontal attack. The "in your face" presentation of immoral lifestyles such as co-habitation, homosexuality, and extra-marital sex; or the political and social pressures that promote materialism, abortion, and no-fault divorce, are but some of the ways *the world* attacks the Army of God. Some of the most potent weapons used by *the world* for these attacks are the news and entertainment media. But the attack is not always frontal.

Consider the flanking movements and ambushes that are used in a more subtle way. An example is the TV show "All In The Family" of a few decades ago. Archie Bunker, the anti-hero, was a world-class bigot, and had obviously been deprived of more enlightened thinking. Isn't it interesting that he took stands against such things as "shacking up" and homosexuality, practices that are clearly condemned in God's Word. *The world's* translation: people who believe in biblical morality are bigots.

Some more recent TV shows that have used a subtle approach in attacking God's Army include "The Practice", "JAG", and "Boston Public". All of these are series which started out with interesting story lines, good acting and compelling plots. It wasn't long, however, before each of these shows began to include sexual immorality in a sympathetic or favorable light. Many soldiers in God's Army have no doubt gotten "hooked" on these and/or other programs that use the same tactics.

The good news here is that we don't have to be defeated by *the world.* We can be like Moses. He had it all: wealth, power, the "good life" and all the other perks that come from being a "top dog" in Pharaoh's court. Hebrews 11:24-25 tells us, however, that *"By faith Moses when he became of age, refused to be called the son of Pharaoh's daughter, choosing rather to suffer affliction with the people of God than to enjoy the passing pleasures of sin."*

Eusebius, the Bishop of Caesarea (c. A.D. 260-339), was one of the first church historians. His writings contain numerous accounts of soldiers in God's Army who, like Moses, *"suffered affliction"* by taking a stand against *the world.* Here's an example:

*"Need I cite the names or numbers of the rest or the varieties of their martyrdoms? Sometimes they were killed with an axe, as was the case in Arabia, or had their legs broken, as those in Cappadocia. At other times they were hung upside down over a slow fire, so that smoke rising from the burning wood suffocated them, as in Mesopotamia. Sometimes noses, ears, and hands were mutilated and the other parts of the body butchered, as was the case in Alexandria."* [i]

In China and several Muslim nations today, many soldiers in God's Army have made that same choice. Some have died as a result. The choice you make today may be as easy as turning off the TV.

And while you may not as yet have suffered the kind of affliction endured by saints throughout the ages, rest assured that if you do serious battle with *the world,* the day will come when you are labeled "a bigot", or "narrow minded", or "holier than thou", and incur a degree of persecution that will test your faith. When that happens, take comfort in the words of Jesus, *"Blessed are you when they revile and persecute you, and say all kinds of evil against you falsely for My sake. Rejoice and be exceedingly glad, for so they persecuted the prophets who were before you"* (Mt. 5:11-12).

As with *the flesh,* this is the time to put into practice what we learned in Basic Training (chapter 3) and begin to use the weapons God has given us (chapter 6) to be victorious in spiritual warfare.

**The devil.** When appearing on a popular TV talk show several years ago, entertainer Pat Boone was questioned by the host (an obvious agnostic) about his faith in God. When Pat made reference to the devil, the host retorted, *"O, I don't believe in the devil."* To this comment, Boone responded with, *"Well, once you believe in God, you'll believe in the devil."* His point, of course, was that Satan and his legions of demons keep so busy attacking the soldiers in God's Army, that they don't have much time to spend harassing unbelievers. It has been said that the devil isn't concerned so much with sending people to hell, as he is in keeping them from being obedient to God.

So, how can one tell when they are dealing with the devil or an evil spirit? In his book, *THE ULTIMATE INTENTION*, author DeVern Fromke identifies four sources of difficulties that mankind faces: (1)God; (2) the enemy; (3) the result of natural forces; and (4) our own deliberate choices.

Fromke uses words such as *oppression* and *hindrance* to describe the tactics of Satan. Acknowledging that it is often difficult to discern the source of such attacks, he adds these words of encouragement:

> *"When we submit our lives wholly to the Lord, we may have assurance that nothing reaches us without His permission.* ***In everything we are able to give thanks****. The need for careful discernment is in itself a source of great blessing, for it keeps us in the place of the humble learner."*[ii]

Besides watching for *oppression* and *hindrance,* as suggested by Fromke, another way of spotting demonic activity is to test the spirits, as directed in 1 John 4:1-3. This is especially useful when dealing with an individual you suspect of being possesed or influenced by an evil spirit. I recall ministering to a troubled young man several years ago, who was unable to say, *"Jesus Christ has come in the flesh."* We immediately took authority over the hindering spirit that was harassing him. The evil spirit was cast out, and the young man received Christ as Lord and Savior.

All of the weapons described in Chapter 6 can be used in battles with demonic forces. These battles will also require full preparation, as outlined in Chapter 7, especially walking in the fulness of the Holy Spirit. The soldier in God's Army who is filled with the Holy Spirit is more likely to be blessed with the gift of *discerning of spirits,* as described in 1 Cor. 12:10. It is interesting to note how Jesus, as well as many of the saints in both old and new testaments, were able to discern evil spirits and identify them by name. A few examples:

Lying spirit – (1 Kings 22:22-23)
Perverse spirit – (Is.19:14)
Spirit of heaviness – (Is. 61:3)
Spirit of harlotry – (Hos. 4:12; 5:4)
Deaf and dumb spirit (Mk. 9:25)
Spirit of infirmity – (Lu. 13:11)
Spirit of divination (Religious spirit) – (Acts 16:16)
Spirit of bondage - (Ro. 8:15)
Spirit of fear – (2 Tim. 1:7)

Other generic terms used in identifying demons include:

Evil spirit – (Acts 19:15-16)
Unclean spirit – (Lu. 8:29)
Foul spirit – (Rev. 18:2)

One final warning when engaging in warfare with *the devil*: remember, he is "sneaky." You may recall that one of the strategies of Satan is to disguise himself as *an angel of light* (2 Cor. 11:14). You may even encounter, as I did once, a demon who does not seem to be particularly harmful. A young man named Chet (not his real name) came to our home one day several years ago, and claimed that a "friendly ghost" was sitting on his shoulder and would not leave. Being new believers at the time, my wife and I took authority over the spirit in the name of Jesus, and commanded it to leave; and according to Chet, the spirit immediately jumped off his shoulder and ran out the door. Real or imagined, such demons can keep a believer from fulfilling his God-given purpose.

For some really good reading on the subtle (and not so subtle) ways that demonic beings can influence believers, I highly recommend THE SCREWTAPE LETTERS , by C. S. Lewis.[iii] This imaginary series of letters from a high ranking devil (Screwtape) to one of his evil errand boys (Wormwood), is humorous as well as informative concerning the strategies of Satan.

**The Combined Enemy Attack.** Whether you're a new recruit or a combat-hardened veteran, if you've seen any service as a soldier in God's Army, you know that more often than not, our spiritual enemies will combine forces to prevent the Kingdom of God from being established or proclaimed. To illustrate how such warfare is waged, we'll look at three specific battles: (1) The Battle In The Workplace; (2) The Battle For Teen Challenge; and (3) The Battle For The Family.

## The Battle In The Workplace

What causes a man (or woman) to step on the backs of others, spread malicious rumors, or engage in other ungodly behavior for the purposes of professional advancement? How is it that happily married men (and women) are so easily drawn into office romances, often resulting in adulterous affairs? And what is it that turns a devoted husband and father into a "workaholic" who can't find time to take his wife to a movie, or attend his kid's ball game? The answer to these and similar questions is some combination of *the world, the flesh, and the devil.* And unfortunately, these spiritual enemies are inflicting many casualties among believers and unbelievers alike.

During my 38 years in the secular workforce, I was fortunate enough to keep from becoming such a casualty. But, the experience was not without conflict. Shortly after going to work for a Fortune 500 company in 1954, I made a list of the levels of management which I planned to attain by the time I reached age 30, 35, 40, etc. culminating in the position of CEO by age 50. In 1970, at age 38, I was offered a job which would advance my career goals ahead of my schedule.

The only problem was that in 1968 I had committed my life to Christ, and my priorities had changed. While considering the job offer, I was confronted with my strong desire for status and recognition, along with a host of other lousy motives. Rationalizing that I could still advance to my boss' job in the future, and not change my field (which the job offer would have required), I turned the promotion down.

In the eyes of *the world,* this was a foolish decision. It earned me a reputation among top management of not being willing to make the sacrifices required to move up the corporate ladder. So, in 1979, when the time came for my boss to leave the company, an interesting thing happened.

Because of my extensive professional experience, I was considered a "shoe-in" for the position of Director of Advertising. But management chose to appoint a temporary, while searching for *"the right man for the job."* After a few months of waiting, I heard from the Lord one morning during my "quiet time." The impression came very clearly, *"You're not going to get the job, but I have something better for you."* And sure enough, within a few weeks, the announcement was made that the new Director of Advertising would be a young man with little experience in the field, but was on a "fast track" for promotion within the company.

Even though the Holy Spirit had prepared me a few weeks earlier, I took the announcement very hard. I felt anger, bitterness, resentment, and a bunch of other ungodly emotions. While driving home from work that day, I had a healthy dose of repentance before I "got the victory", and started looking forward to the *"something better"* that the Lord had mentioned.

In the days that followed, I complained to the Lord one morning that I no longer had the incentive of promotion to spur me on in the performance of my job. The Holy Spirit immediately brought to my mind the verse, *"Whatever you do, do your work heartily as for the Lord rather than for men"* (Col. 3:23). That word became **life** to me that day, so when I got to the office, I wrote it down on a card and placed it in a prominent position on my desk. It is still on my desk today. But that was just the beginning of the *"something better."*

During the next several years the company was either reorganizing or "downsizing" on a regular basis. My job was eliminated three years in a row. One year I dropped five job grades. The next year I was raised six grades. Another passage of scripture became **life** to me, Psalm 75:6-7, *"For promotion cometh neither from the east, nor from the west, nor from the south, but God is the judge; He putteth down one and setteth up another."*

As God used the job situation to deal with my pride and self-sufficiency, while teaching me about humility, grace and His peace, it became apparent that the *"something better"* He had in mind was another step to *conform me into the image of Jesus* (Ro.8:28-29).

The battle in the workplace finds *the world, the flesh, and the devil* constantly mounting a strong attack against the soldiers in God's Army.

## The Battle For Teen Challenge

In Chapter One, we mentioned briefly how Teen Challenge was founded in 1958. What was not said there is that this ministry has a cure rate of over 80%. That is, for those completing the Teen

Challenge program, over 80% are "drug-free" after two years. That kind of success is phenomenal when compared to government and secular drug treatment programs.

Some may never have heard of Teen Challenge, but with results like that you can be sure that our spiritual enemies have taken notice. *The world* makes it easy to get drugs; *the flesh*, once hooked, doesn't want to give them up; and *the devil* will do everything he can to keep his victims enslaved. That's why in 1971, we were engaged in a fierce spiritual battle to establish a Teen Challenge Center in Syracuse, NY.

To help tell the story, I'll quote from an article that appeared in the December 14, 1971 issue of the SYRACUSE NEW TIMES, a publication aimed at college and university students and faculty. *"Syracuse has a history of refusing residence to 'liberal' programs. Recently the Common Council voted down proposals for Brighton Family Center, a half-way house on Kirk Street and a home for troubled girls. Councilmen, representing their constituencies, voted down these programs because the residents of the neighborhoods for which the programs were intended did not want them. Last week, though, was a different story. On Dec. 4 the Council approved a program for drug addicts, Teen Challenge Inc., for the Furman Street area. It was a remarkable inconsistency in pattern for the Council because the Furman Street people do not want a home for drug abusers in their neighborhood."*

The *spirit of fear* was so strong in the meeting described above, you could almost touch it. I vividly remember praying, along with others involved in the Teen Challenge ministry, for God to bind the *spirit of fear* operating in the Furman Street residents, and to loose the *spirit of truth* into the minds of the members of the Common Council. God apparently did both of those things, as approval was given to proceed with establishing the Center.

The reporter for the NEW TIMES included several disparaging and cynical comments in her article. Here is part of what she wrote about some comments I made: *"...a handsome astronaut-type who had been sitting quite still with a peaceful look on his face, stood. He said he is the father of four children, three of whom are in the drug age, that he has visited three Teen Challenge facilities and was very impressed, and that most importantly, two days ago was the first Sunday of Advent and Christians the world over should save their fellow men. He said he has been transformed by the spirit of Jesus Christ, and felt it was time we called upon Him to solve the drug problem. If he said he was the mother of four children he couldn't have aroused more empathy than he did. He sat down, either lobotomized or at peace, and with no change of expression and no movement of limbs, watched patiently as the Common Council called upon Jesus Christ to solve the drug problem – in someone else's backyard, of course."*

Although written with a heavy dose of sarcasm, I was flattered by the description of my remarks. After all, Christians are supposed to model peace, since we serve *the Prince of peace.* As for the lobotomy, I understand that is a surgical procedure designed to alter the brain – and when Jesus Christ came into my life, He definitely changed the way I think. Whether or not I said all the things she reported, I was pleased to use *the word of my testimony* (see Chapter 6) as a spiritual weapon.

But that was only the beginning of the battle for Teen Challenge in Syracuse. During the years that followed, there were struggles for finances, problems with some of the students, and even the need to dismiss one of the staff when it was discovered that he was a homosexual. Today, the Syracuse Teen Challenge Center is still going strong. During over 30 years of operation, hundreds of young men have been set free from addictive lifestyles. Many of these have gone on to the Teen Challenge Training Center in Rehrersburg, PA, where they have received additional rehabilitation as well as spiritual and vocational training. The result has been the equipping of many more soldiers in the Army of God.

## The Battle For The Family

When God said, *"It is not good for man to be alone"* (Gen.2:18), it was obvious that He had the family in mind. What happened after that makes it clear that His idea of a family was a husband (male), a wife (female), and children. Throughout scripture we see the family unit as basic to the plans and purposes of God for mankind. His Word even describes His relationship with us as that of a Father and His children. And the relationship of Christ and the Church is portrayed as that of a bridegroom and a bride. So it is not surprising that *the world, the flesh and the devil* should launch an all-out attack on this God-ordained, basic unit of society, the family.

The entertainment media (representing *the world*) continually bombard us with images of unbiblical family "alternatives", not to mention the appeal to the lusts of *the flesh.* And, of course, *the devil* is the instigator of much of the filth that floods our homes through our TV sets. This truth is seen symbolically in Rev. 12:15 which says, *"The serpent (the devil) poured water like a river out of his mouth after the woman (the Church) to sweep her away with the flood."*

The news media and the scientific/medical community also get involved with the attack. Consider the following excerpt from an article in the Feb. 18, 2002 issue of U.S. NEWS & WORLD REPORT , under the heading <u>Gay parents endorsed by kids' docs</u>: *"In many gay families, two parents drive carpools and comfort fussy babies. But only one of them – the birth or adoptive mother or father – is the legal parent. Last week, the American Academy of Pediatrics called for a change. It wants state laws to permit gays to adopt their partners' children, noting that kids raised by same-sex parents do as well as those in traditional families."*

Make no mistake about it, the homosexual agenda is a real threat to the traditional family. Add to that the activities of the abortion lobby, along with *the world's* acceptance of "no-fault divorce", and it becomes obvious that The Family is under heavy spiritual attack.

Many soldiers in God's Army have gotten involved in local issues affecting the family. Thousand of others are members and/or supporters of organizations such as Christian Coalition, Concerned Women For America, and similar groups that are fighting the battle for the family through legal, governmental and other channels. Perhaps God has been speaking to you about getting involved in this particular battle.

In 1969, our family moved from Middlebury, VT to the Syracuse, NY area. It was a hard move for our children, especially for the oldest, who had just become a teenager. Although I was a new Christian at the time, I could sense that there were spiritual forces attacking our family through our children. Within a year after moving, I attended a men's retreat, during which I came across this verse of scripture that I instantly claimed as a promise from God: *"But thus saith the Lord...I will contend with him that contendeth with thee and I will save thy children*" (Is. 49:25). It may have been King James

English, and it may have been slightly out of context, but for me it was God's Word – and I held on to it tightly. Today, thanks to the faithfulness of God, all four of our children are following the Lord and are attending Bible-believing churches.

The battle for the family can be won. But victory will not come without making good use of all the weapons and resources that God has provided for the soldiers in His Army.

The three battles described above are typical of those that soldiers in God's Army may be called on to fight. Whether your battle is today or tomorrow - whether it's a frontal attack, a flanking maneuver or an ambush - whether you're on the defense or the offense - remember, *the battle is not your, it is the Lord's.*

~~~~~~~~~~
~~~~~~~~~~

## DISCUSSION GUIDE FOR CHAPTER EIGHT

1. What could King David have done that might have prevented his sin against Bathsheba and Uriah?

2. What are some ways you can distinguish between an attack from *the devil* and an attack from *the flesh* or *the world?*

3. List some of the steps a soldier in God's army should take after suffering a defeat caused by yielding to temptation.

ENDNOTES

---

[i] EUSEBIUS-The Church History
Copyright © 1999 by Paul L. Maier
Publisher: Kregel Publications, PO Box 2607, Grand Rapids, MI 49501
[ii] THE ULTIMATE INTENTION - by DeVern F. Fromke
Copyright © 1963 - seventh printing, September, 1974
Publisher: Sure Foundation, Box 74 – Rt.2, Cloverdale, IN 46120
[iii] THE SCREWTAPE LETTERS - by C. S. Lewis
Copyright © 1959, 1961
Publisher: Macmillan Publishing Co., Inc. 866 3rd Ave., NY, NY 10022

# CHAPTER NINE

## WALKING IN VICTORY

*"Then comes the end when He delivers the Kingdom to God the Father, when He puts an end to all rule and all authority and power. For He must reign till He has put all enemies under His feet. Thanks be to God who gives us the victory through our Lord Jesus Christ"* 1 Cor. 15:24-25, 57).

**PEACE**, screamed the banner headlines of newspapers throughout the world on August 15, 1945. The lead story on page one of the PHILADELPHIA INQUIRER, describing the end of World War II, began this way:

> *"WASHINGTON, Aug. 14 – The war is over. Japan has surrendered unconditionally,and Allied forces on land and sea have been ordered to cease firing."*

Now, the United States and its allies had to learn once again what it means to *walk in victory*. And if there is one lesson this nation has learned throughout its history, it is that *peace does not necessarily mean the absence of conflict.* Limited wars in Korea, VietNam, the Persian Gulf and other parts of the world reflect the presence of ongoing military conflict. Of a more pervasive nature, however, are problems such as a fluctuating economy, declining morality, politics, racism and other social ills, to mention just a few. Indeed, it has been a long time since any serious presidential candidate in the U.S. has been able to run on a record of *Peace and Prosperity.*

So, what can we, as soldiers in the Army of God, learn from all this? The obvious answer may sound a bit familiar: *peace does not necessarily mean the absence of conflict.* You see, our enemies are still out there – and, they have not yet surrendered. The difference now is that we know our enemies have been defeated. Jesus told us that He has overcome *the world*; He defeated *the devil* when He went to the cross; and He gave us His Spirit so that we no longer have to walk in *the flesh.* Besides applying what we learned in Basic Training; and in addition to making use of our spiritual weapons, there are a few key principles that will help us to WALK IN VICTORY.

### Principle No. 1 – Confidence in God

We have stated that whether in military affairs or spiritual warfare, *peace does not necessarily mean the absence of conflict.* So what does *peace* mean? For the soldier in God's Army, *peace is an abiding confidence in the presence and power of God in my life.* It is an awareness of His sovereignty, a sensitivity to His presence, and an intimate, moment-to-moment communion with Him, regardless of my circumstances. This definition of *peace* is not a confidence in my own abilities or level of spiritual maturity – but a total trust in who God is and what He is able to do in and through me. As a word of encouragement to believers in Philippi,

Paul said he was *"...**confident** of this very thing, that He who has begun a good work in you will complete it until the day of Jesus Christ"* (Phil. 1:6).

It is this kind of confidence that the writer of the letter to the Hebrews had in mind when he penned such words as, *"Let us come boldly before the throne of grace, that we may obtain mercy and find grace to help in time of need"* (Heb. 4:16), and *"So we may boldly say, 'The Lord is my helper; I will not fear. What can man do to me?'"* (Heb. 13:6). To have this kind of confidence in God requires experiential knowledge of *who we are in Christ.* (A partial explanation of this can be found on pages 66 through 68, where we discussed *The Word of Our Testimony* as one of the weapons in our spiritual arsenal.)

Such experiential knowledge is seen and encouraged in numerous passages of scripture: *"Be still and **know*** (not just hope) *that I am God"* (Ps. 46:10); *"...they shall all **know** Me* (not just know about Me), *from the least of them to the greatest of them, says the Lord"* (Jer. 31:34); *"You shall **know*** (not just suspect) *the truth and the truth shall set you free"* (Jn. 8:32); *"These things I have written...that you may **know*** (not just wish) *that you have eternal life..."* (1 Jn. 5:13). There are many more such passages that can help you build the kind of confidence in God that will enable you to *walk in victory.*

At this point, you are probably thinking that

*having confidence in God* is really just having a strong faith. You are right!! *"This is the victory that has overcome the world – our faith"* (1 Jn. 5:4).

**Principle No. 2 – Death to Self**

For years, I puzzled over the passage of scripture in chapter 12 of John's gospel (vs.20-25), where Philip and Andrew come to the Lord with the good news that there are some Greeks attending one of the feasts who have expressed a desire to *see Jesus*. The Lord's response once seemed to me to be almost rude, in that He apparently ignored the Greeks, and started talking about a grain of wheat falling into the ground and dying.

Finally, the light came on. By explaining that a grain of wheat must first die before it can bring forth a bountiful crop, Jesus illustrates for His disciples that in order to gain eternal life, we must give up our worldly self-life. When we do this, it is then that the Greeks (representing those outside of the Church) will be able to *see Jesus*.

The Apostle Paul understood that death to self was a key to *walking in victory*. Consider a few of his well known exhortations on the subject::

*"For to me to live is Christ, and to die is gain"* (Phil.1:21);

*"...I die daily"* (I Cor. 15:31);

*"For while we live, we are always being given up to death for Jesus' sake, so that the life of Jesus may be manifest in our mortal flesh"* (2 Cor. 4:11).

Right now you may be thinking that all this talk about dying to self sounds rather morose. In reality, however, it is not. Author and Pastor John Piper puts it this way, *"The Calvary road with Jesus is not a joyless road. It is a painful one, but a profoundly happy one. When we choose the fleeting pleasures of comfort and security over the sacrifices of missions and evangelism and ministry and love, we choose against joy. We reject the springs whose waters never fail (Is. 58:11). The happiest people in the world are the people who experience the mystery of 'Christ in them, the hope of glory' (Col.1:27), satisfying their deep longings and freeing them to extend the afflictions of Christ through their own suffering to the world."* [i] Are you beginning to see how dying to self is an essential element of *walking in victory?*

Several years ago at an annual Teen Challenge fund raising banquet in Syracuse, NY, the guest speaker was Don Wilkerson. Don is the brother of Teen Challenge founder, Dave Wilkerson, and at that time was director of the Brooklyn, NY Teen Challenge Center. During the course of his remarks, he told about observing one of his staff talking with one of the students in the program. When the student complimented the staff member by telling him how much he looked up to him, the staff member replied by saying, *"Don't look to me, look to Jesus."* Don later took the staff member aside, and reminded him that if the students don't see Jesus in him, they may not see Jesus at all. Sound familiar? It should, because that's the same lesson Jesus was teaching His disciples who brought Greeks to Him, wishing to *see Jesus.*

This principle of *death to self* is perhaps best expressed in the words of Jesus, when He said, *"If anyone wants to be a follower of mine, let him deny himself and take up his cross and follow Me"* (Mt. 16:24).

This commandment, referred to by many Bible teachers as *the way of the cross,* has unfortunately been misinterpreted by some to mean doing things we don't want to do, out of a sense of obligation, in hopes that it will somehow please a strict and demanding God. *"I suppose caring for my sick mother-in-law is the cross I have to bear"* is a classic example of this wrong thinking.

The true meaning of *the way of the cross* is when we *willingly* and *joyfully* do those things which we know will please our loving heavenly Father, rather than what once may have pleased ourselves. This might include visiting the sick rather than staying home to watch TV, or even turning down a promotion because it would take too much time away from family. *The way of the cross* definitely leads to *death to self,* which in turn enables the soldier in God's Army to *walk in victory.*

## Principle No. 3 – Putting First Things First

When God gave the ten commandments to Moses on Mount Sinai, He began with, *"Thou shall have no other gods before Me"* (Ex. 20:3). When one of the scribes asked Jesus which was the greatest commandment, the Lord rephrased this by saying, *"The first is 'Hear O Israel: The Lord our God, the Lord is one; and you shall love the Lord your God with all your heart, and with all your soul, and with all your mind, and with all your strength'"* (Mk. 12:29-30).

Understanding that God (the creator and sustainer of the universe) loves us can be a bit overwhelming. For us to love Him, however, is a little easier, simply because He has done so much for us. But it raises some interesting questions: Does God really need our love? And, what does it mean to love Him *with all our heart, soul, mind and strength?*

Author and Pastor John Piper makes this observation: *"To love God does not mean to meet His needs, but rather to delight in Him and be captivated by His glorious power and grace, and to value Him above all other things on earth."*[ii]

At a Promise Keepers Conference I attended a few years ago, Pastor Joe Garlington of Pittsburgh, was addressing the topic of having a personal relationship with Jesus. He introduced his remarks by saying, *"The main thing - is to make the main thing - the main thing."* That simple but profound statement really spoke to me.

It is truly a fantastic experience to see a sinner come to know the Lord and enter into a love relationship with Him. When this happens, the new believer often says something like, *"Now God has first place in my life."* A statement such as this is commendable. When job, or possessions, or a family member occupy *first place* in one's life, it is a big step to change that number one priority to God.

In marriage counseling, the *Relational Pyramid* (see Figure 3) is often used to help husbands and wives see the value of placing God at the center of their marriage. The reason for this is that only God can meet our basic human needs for security and significance; and when we rely on our mate to meet these needs, sooner or later we will be disappointed.

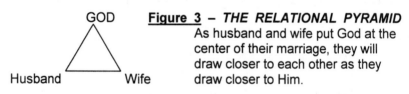

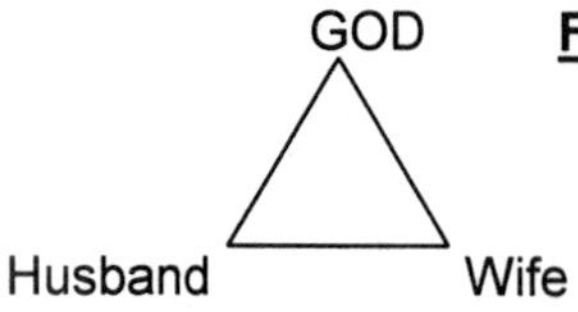


**<u>Figure 3</u> – *THE RELATIONAL PYRAMID***
As husband and wife put God at the center of their marriage, they will draw closer to each other as they draw closer to Him.

While the idea of putting Christ *first* in my life is a positive step, there is one drawback of doing so. If I make decisions such as Christ is *number one,* family is *number two,* job is *number three,* etc., then at some time in the future, I may decide to change those priorities around, and something other than God takes *first place.* To keep this from happening, allow me to suggest a different way of establishing priorities. Paul said, *"...Christ is our life..."* (Col.3:4) and, *"For to me to live is Christ..."* (Ph. 1:21). These statements make it clear that **Christ is much more than *first place* in my life, He is the very *source of my life*;** and everything else – job, relationships, possessions, hobbies, etc. are funneled into my day-to-day activities through Him who is *the source of my life.*

This way, whatever God wants to be my top priority, at any given time, is decided by Him, not me. To the extent that I am able to do this, I am observing the First Commandment, and *putting first things first.*

## Principle No. 4 – Embrace Change

It has often been said that God loves us just the way that we are, BUT He loves us too much to let us stay that way. The truth of this statement is born out all through scripture.

In the Old Testament, Jeremiah describes how God would bring judgement on the tribe of Moab because they refused to change. Using an illustration from the process of making wine, he says, *"Moab has been at ease from his youth. He has settled on his dregs, and has not been emptied from vessel to vessel. Nor has he gone into captivity. Therefore his taste remained in him, and his scent has not changed"* (Jer. 48:11). The judgement that God would bring on Moab is described in the following verses, which give a graphic picture of how God can bring change in our lives. When we refuse to yield to the process of change – it's not a pretty sight.

For the soldier in God's Army, change begins the moment we receive Christ as Lord and Savior (2 Cor. 5:17). Romans 8:29 makes it clear that God's purpose for every believer is that we become like Jesus. (The last time I checked, I wasn't quite there yet). Paul describes the process like this:*"...we all, with unveiled face, beholding as in a mirror the glory of the Lord, are being transformed into the same image from glory to glory..."* (2 Cor. 3:18).

Both Paul and John talk about that one final change that will be made in each of us when Christ returns. John says, *"...it has not yet been revealed what we shall be, but we know that when He is revealed, we shall be like Him, for we shall see Him as He is"* (1Jn. 3:2). In 1 Corinthians 15, Paul describes the return of Jesus and His final victory over the last enemy, *death.* Twice in that passage, he says *we shall be changed* (vs. 51, 52).

To say that change is not always comfortable is a huge understatement. The truth is, it is often quite painful. Much of what I have learned about *change* comes from a tape I listened to years ago, by popular Bible teacher, Bob Mumford. Here's a brief summary of some of the main points from that teaching:

1. One of the greatest hindrances to change is

tradition – especially the traps we fall into as a result of our doctrinal and theological beliefs. (We've always done it this way. But, my denomination teaches...,etc.)

2. A proper spiritual attitude about change includes:
   (A) Be seeking and move out by faith (He.11:8-10; Mt. 7:7);
   (B) Be open to new revelation, as long as it is scripturally sound;
   (C) Jesus and His purposes first – all else secondary (Mt. 6:33).

3. Change may involve job, geography, understanding, circumstances, life-style, relationships, etc.

4. After you've made change number one, get ready for number two.

*Walking in victory* is definitely going to involve yielding to and embracing change.

**Principle No. 5 – Have An Honest Heart**

As I shared with a friend one day that I was in the process of writing a book on *spiritual warfare,* she asked me if I felt under any greater spiritual attack as a result of this project. I replied that I had not been aware of any increase in the level of enemy activity. As I was reflecting on that response a few days later, a passage of scripture came to mind which I believe is one reason for my apparent ability to ward off assaults from the enemy: *"Trust in the Lord with all thine heart, and lean not unto thine own understanding. In all thy ways acknowledge Him, and He shall direct thy paths"* (Pr. 3:5-6).

In chapter three we pointed out that many of our spiritual battles take place in *the mind,* and that we need to use *the mind of Christ* as a spiritual weapon (see pages 68-70). All three of our spiritual enemies can launch an attack against our mind. *The world,* via the entertainment media, will tell us that sex outside of marriage is perfectly normal and acceptable. *The flesh,* with its appeal to our desire for pleasure, makes yielding to carnal inclinations a relatively easy and convenient possibility. And *the devil* just loves to plant ideas in our mind that will cause us to step out of the will of God.

So, regardless of where the attack comes from, I am trying to learn to *acknowledge Him* when faced with temptation. This means I speak the name of Jesus (mentally if not verbally), and say *"Lord, I acknowledge You as Lord of my life, and I am trusting You to direct my path in the way You want me to walk."* When I do this, and do it with *an honest heart,* the result is almost always *victory.*

The operative words here are *trusting with all my heart,* and *acknowledging Him.* Jesus talked about the importance of *an honest heart* when He interpreted for His disciples the meaning of the parable of the sower. After explaining why the seed that fell along the wayside, and on the rock, and among the thorns, were all unfruitful, He said that the seed that fell *"...on the good ground are they, which in an honest and good heart, having heard the word, keep it, and bring forth fruit with patience"* (Lu. 8:15). Here we see that an *honest heart* is one that is open and sensitive to God and to His word.

Scripture makes it clear that this is what God desires in His people when it says, *"For the eyes of the Lord move to and fro throughout the earth that He may strongly support those whose heart is completely His"* (2 Chron. 16:9); and, *"...you will seek Me and find Me, when you search for Me with all your heart"* (Jer. 29:13).

During the decade of the nineties, God moved in a powerful way among men through an organization called PROMISE KEEPERS (PK for short). Encouraging men to be a Godly influence in their homes, churches, work places and communities, PK uses the theme *Men of Integrity.* The implications of this theme are obvious: in order to keep the commitments that a *Promise Keeper* makes, it requires *an honest heart.* And so it is for every soldier in the Army of God – male or female, young or old, regardless of skin color, social standing or denomination, God is looking for *an honest heart.* He wants you to be honest with yourself, with your fellow man, and above all, with Him. If you can do that, you are well on your way to *walking in victory.*

It is interesting to note how much the Bible has to say not only about *being victorious,* but also about *walking.* As soldiers in the Army of God, we are instructed to *walk...*

...by faith (2 Cor. 5:7)
...in newness of life (Ro. 6:4)
...by the Spirit (Ga. 5:16)
...honestly (1 Thes. 4:12)
...in love (Eph. 5:2)
...worthy of our calling (Eph.4:1)
...in the light (1 Jn. 1:7)
...in wisdom (Col. 4:5)
...in truth (3 Jn. 4)

And the five principles we have discussed here, if properly applied, can help us walk according to the Word of God, which means *walking in victory:*

1. Confidence in God
2. Death to self
3. Putting first things first
4. Embrace Change
5. Have an honest heart

Through your own personal experience, and through your study of God's Word, you can no doubt find other scriptural principles that will help you be a victorious soldier in the Army of God.

~~~~~~~~~~~
~~~~~~~~~~~

## DISCUSSION GUIDE FOR CHAPTER NINE

1. On a scale of 1 to10 (10 being excellent, and 1 being poor), rate yourself on the following principles for *walking in victory:*

| Principle | My Rating |
|---|---|
| - Confidence in God | _____ |
| - Death to self | _____ |
| - Putting first things first | _____ |
| - Embracing change | _____ |
| - An honest heart | _____ |

2. What steps do I need to take to improve my *walking in victory* ratings?

_______________________________________________

_______________________________________________

3. What are some other principles I have learned for *walking in victory*?

_______________________________________________

_______________________________________________

ENDNOTES

[i] DESIRING GOD – Meditations Of A Christian Hedonist
by John Piper (pg. 236)
Copyright © 1986 by Multnomah Press
Copyright © 1996 byJohn Piper
Publisher: Questar Publishers Inc. PO Box 1720,Sisters,OR 97759

[ii] DESIRING GOD (pg.. 259)

# EPILOGUE

In our Prologue, we began with Joshua and the Israelites entering the Promised Land. It seems only fitting, therefore, that we conclude with Joshua. Approximately 24 years have passed since Israel crossed the Jordan. They had done battle with the Amorites, the Hittites, the Perizzites, the Jebusites, the Hivites, and a whole bunch of other *ites;* just as we, the soldiers in God's Army, fight against the Pride*ites*, the Lust*ites*, the Fear*ites*, the Anger*ites*, the Jealousy*ites*, the Gossip*ites*, and all the other enemies of our soul.

Knowing that he will soon die, Joshua says, *"I am going the way of all the earth, and you know in all your hearts and in all your souls that not one word of all the words which the Lord your God spoke concerning you has failed..."* (Josh. 23:14). Besides pointing out the faithfulness of God, Joshua also reminds the Israelites that if they wish to continue to receive God's blessings, they will need to continue to choose His ways rather than the ways of their fathers or of their enemies (Josh. 24:14-15).

Toward the end of his farewell address, he boldly proclaims, *"...as for me and my house, we will serve the Lord"* (Josh. 24:15), a statement of intent repeated by countless numbers of soldiers in God's Army throughout succeeding generations.

The entire book of Joshua offers every soldier in God's Army a magnificent study in spiritual warfare. It is a book of conquest and victory – a book of salvation and deliverance – a book of possessing our inheritance – a book of God's holiness and faithfulness – and most of all, a book of learning to know and trust God in all our spiritual battles.

These themes found in Joshua are repeated throughout scripture. One of my favorites is, *"If God be for us, who can be against us? …in all these things,* ***we are more than conquerors*** *through Him that loved us"* (Ro. 8:31, 37). The concept of being *more than a conqueror* is a promise from God that I surely want to lay hold of in every aspect of my life. I trust you do also.

One final scripture, without which no study in spiritual warfare would be complete: *"When the enemy shall come in like a flood, the Spirit of the Lord shall lift up a standard against him* (Is. 59:19-KJV). Webster defines *standard* three ways:

(1) A flag or banner used as an emblem of a military unit;
(2) Something established for use as a rule or basis of comparison;
(3) An upright support.

It matters not whether the enemy is *the world, the flesh* or *the devil,* as soldiers in the Army of God, we need to call on the Holy Spirit to help us lift up *our standard,* the cross of Jesus (Jn. 3:14), to a world in need of salvation. We also need to establish the standard of His Word *as the rule and basis for comparison* when examining the way we live. And finally, each soldier in God's Army must be *an upright support,* or as the prophet Isaiah expressed it, *"...that they might be called trees of righteousness, the planting of the Lord, that He might be glorified"* (Is. 61:3).

## ABOUT THE AUTHOR

Born and raised in New Rochelle, New York, Frank Hummel grew up in the Presbyterian faith. After graduating from Cornell University in 1954, he spent two years on active duty at the Infantry School at Fort Benning, GA.

Following his military service, Frank worked for a large agribusiness firm, spending most of his career in the field of marketing communications. He and his wife, Betty, made their home at various times in Ithaca, NY, Middlebury, VT, the Syracuse, NY area, and are currently retired in Virginia.

In 1968 Frank had a life-changing encounter with Jesus Christ. Since then he has held leadership positions in several para-church organizations, as well as serving as an elder and teacher in a number of local church fellowships. He currently volunteers in a Christian counseling ministry.

The Hummels have four grown children and nine grandchildren.

~~~~~~~~~~~~

Frank is available on occasion to speak to church groups or other organizations. Contact information may be found on page 133.
~~~~~~~~~~~~

## To order additional copies of

*A Soldier in God's Army*

**Order From Publisher:**

Have your credit card ready and call: Toll free: (866) 484-6184
You may also log onto their website at: **www.csnbooks.com**

**Order From Author:**

**Phone:** 540-721-6539 **Email:** frankhumel@charter.net
(*A Soldier In God's Army* as subject)
**US Mail:** Fill out form below and send with check made payable to:

Frank Hummel
578 Island Pointe Ln., Moneta, VA. 24121

***Frank Hummel welcomes your inquires regarding speaking engagements.***
He can be contacted at address above.

---

Name:______________________________________
Address:____________________________________
City:________________State:________Zip:________
Phone:_____________________________________

Send $9.95* each, plus $2.50 S&H **
* Virgina residents please add 4.5% tax.
****Shipping:** 2-4 books - $3.80; 5-8 books - $5.70; 9-12 books $6.90
**Contact author for special pricing for Churches and Ministries.**

| Qty. | Description | Price | Total |
|---|---|---|---|
| | A Soldier in God's Army | $9.95 | |
| | | | |
| Shipping and Handling (look above for pricing) | | | |
| | | | |
| Grand Total | | | $ |